THE GOOD
Opera
CD GUIDE

THE GOOD Opera CD GUIDE

JOHN CARGHER

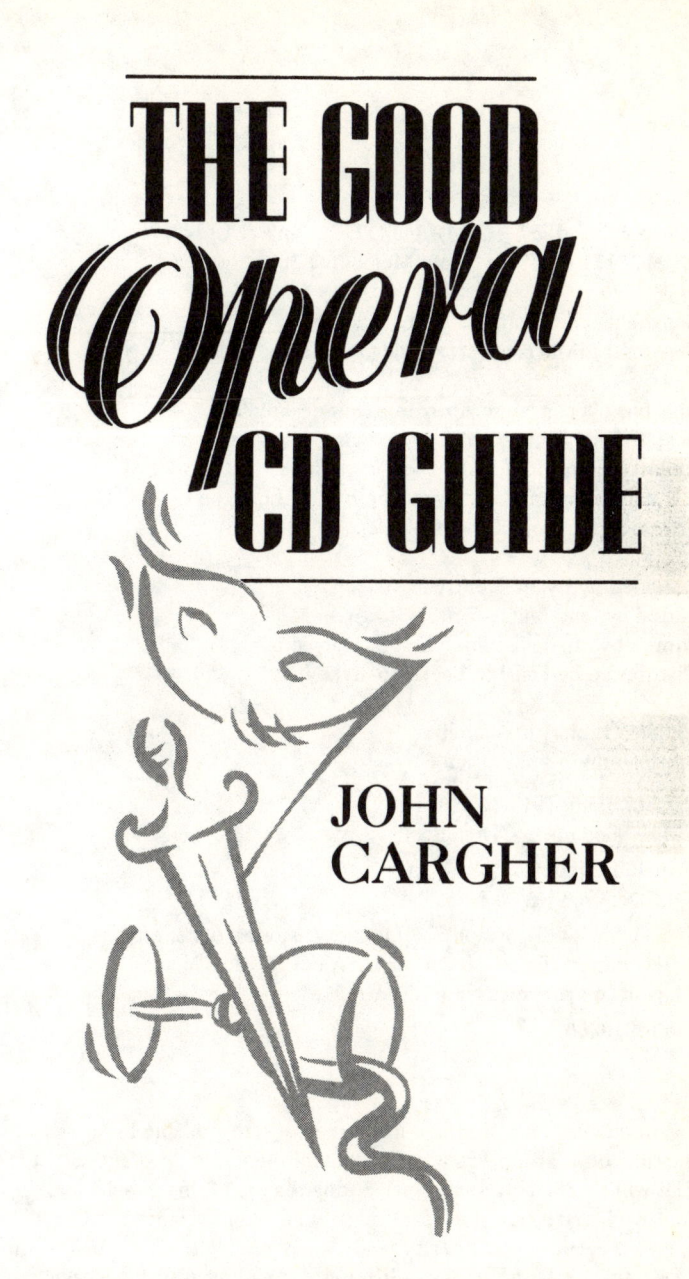

ANNE O'DONOVAN

First published in 1995 by Anne O'Donovan Pty Ltd
Level 3, 171 La Trobe Street Melbourne 3000

Copyright text© John Cargher 1995
Copyright in the concept© Anne O'Donovan 1995

This book is copyright. Apart from fair dealing for the purpose of private study, research, criticism or review, as permitted under the Copyright Act, no part may be reproduced by any process without the written permission of the publisher.

Designed by Lynn Twelftree
Edited by Jane Angus, Writers Reign
Printed by Australian Print Group, Maryborough
Distributed by Penguin Books Australia Ltd

National Library of Australia
Cataloguing-in-publication entry

Cargher, John, 1919–.
 The good opera CD guide.

 Includes index.
 ISBN 0 908476 86 8.

 1. Opera — discography. 2. Operas — stories, plots, etc. 3. Compact discs — Reviews. I. Title. II. Title: Good opera compact disc guide.

016.78210266

Note: The CDs recommended in this guide were available in Australia at the time of printing. The author and publisher do not guarantee that the CDs will be available at all times during the life of this publication.
We have listed a selection of recommended record retailers in Australia and in New Zealand. New Zealand readers may be able to obtain hard-to-find CDs from the Australian shops listed, if they are unavailable locally.

Contents

Introduction	8
Using this book	13
Sample entry	17

Operas on CD	19
Great singers of the past	143
24 great singers on CD opera sets	147
The mixed CD recital	164

LISTS
The basic collection	31

The Top Ten
Sopranos in operas on CD	42
Tenors in operas on CD	62
Baritones in operas on CD	73
Mezzo-sopranos in operas on CD	107
Basses in operas on CD	119
Tenor arias	165
Soprano arias	165
Baritone arias	165
Mezzo-soprano arias	166
Bass arias	166
Operatic ensembles	166

INDEXES
Index of artists	169
Index of most popular arias, duets, etc.	179
Index of operas	182

Recommended retailers	187

BUY THIS BOOK

if you have heard 'Nessun dorma' and other familiar arias but don't know from which opera they come, or if you love fine singing but don't know how to find your way to new or old recordings of your favourite works.

DON'T BUY THIS BOOK

if you are looking for a comprehensive list of all operas available on CD, serious analytical dissertations on their history and musical values, or if you value the sound you hear more than the musical aspects of a recording.

Introduction

Recent years have seen what has commonly been called the 'opera explosion', the sudden rise to unprecedented popularity of an art form which used to be considered the prerogative of the upper classes and incomprehensible to the average person. Quite possibly, the development of modern musical theatre and the improvement in the visual aspects of opera productions has led people to realise that there is no fundamental difference between the works of Andrew Lloyd-Webber or Stephen Sondheim and those of Puccini or Mozart.

The increased popularity of opera resulted in a stream of complete opera recordings in the days of the long-playing record, which became a torrent when CDs took over. Before 1950 the average number of annual recordings of complete stage works was one or less! After 1950 dozens appeared each year on LP. Now, since the arrival of CDs, not a month passes without the issue of five, six or a dozen complete opera recordings. Literally hundreds of such works, not counting discs of highlights, are in the current catalogues, and the most popular operas can be bought in twenty or more different CD sets; there are twenty *Toscas* and twenty *Traviatas*, and the ones featuring the most famous artists are not necessarily the best.

There is no 'best' recording

This book is designed to give basic information about the operas which contain the arias heard daily on radio and television, often as parts of advertisements. The most famous arias do not necessarily come out of the most popular operas, but it is the arias which are responsible for the opera explosion. Each entry in this book is headed by a list of the arias contained in the work. There is also an index to the most popular arias at the end of the book.

There is no such thing as one specific CD of many musical works which is 'the best'. Personal tastes may make one opera set more desirable than another; the adulation of opera stars is as great today as it was in the days of Caruso. The only difference is that the millions of fans of Caruso have turned into billions for the current Big Three—Carreras, Domingo and Pavarotti. But even a manic Pavarotti fan who wishes to buy a complete opera starring the great tenor must consider the contribution of the soprano and the baritone and the conductor and the recording quality and much else.

Unlike most CD guides, this book concentrates on the quality of the singers rather than the quality of the conductor. The newcomer to opera will not appreciate the finer points of the orchestral nuances. Where the contribution of conductor is particularly noteworthy in the success of any set, this is indicated in the commentary.

Operatic travel guide

I have selected recordings of complete works and/or highlights on the basis of general acceptability to the average person. The experienced opera lover will not need to read this book. It is rather like a musical travel guide; we all know which buildings or natural wonders we would like to see, but what else can we take in at the same time? Is it worth travelling so far at such expense if there is only one sight to see in the end? Of course not. Any tour package is built around a number of features and every opera has more than one Taj Mahal or Niagara Falls.

The famous 'Nessun dorma' is the perfect example. Puccini's *Turandot*, in which it appears, is not a 'popular' opera; you have to wait nearly two hours before those familiar strains arrive on the scene. There are actually four other arias in the work which have been recorded extensively on their own, but they will be familiar only to experienced record collectors, and even some of those may find the extended periods of not very Puccini-like music which separates them an initially boring landscape.

My selections do not appear in order of excellence; too many factors are involved. The virtues of each are offset by some failings, which in other sets may be virtues. All sets listed are acceptable to any potential buyer.

What is an opera?

Opera is the Latin plural of *opus*, a word which has entered our language to define a musical composition; Beethoven's fifth symphony is his *Op. 67*. The word *opus* translates as 'work'. The plural *opera* translates as 'works'. Thus an opera is a collection of works by not only the composer, but the librettist, the designer, the director and the performers.

Opera is drama with music, not music with drama. Nobody has ever written the music for an opera and added the words afterwards. The composer needs the words for inspiration. Yet Antonio Salieri, of *Amadeus* fame, wrote an opera called *Prima la musica e poi le parole* ('first the music and then the words') and Richard Strauss' *Capriccio* is equally concerned with the question of which comes first, the words or the music. Salieri and Strauss were both composers favouring the Salieri title, but Strauss in the twentieth century had the good sense not to resolve the question, only to ask it. Is it really coincidence that neither work is as popular as any by Puccini or Verdi?

Listening to the music of an opera on CD deprives the buyer of the visual aspect of the art, a handicap which is only partly overcome by the usually, but not always, supplied libretto containing translation, synopsis and often useful background notes. What must not be forgotten is that in its original form everybody wanted to see (and hear, of course) the latest opera, because the story being told on stage was as new and as interesting as the music. For every opera we know today hundreds were written which have disappeared completely. Many were a substantial success initially, because their dramatic content, sung in a language understood by the audience, was a novelty.

What we see in today's opera houses survived on the strength of the music, of course. Nobody will stage the play on which *Rigoletto*, for example, was based. The author of that was the famous Victor Hugo. Which raises the question: where is the borderline between operas and musicals? The same Victor Hugo wrote the story on which the musical *Les Miserables* is based. Neither work has any spoken dialogue, but one was written in 1851 and the other in 1980. Same author, different music, but identical in dramatic, theatrical and musical terms. I am happy to see that magazines like *Gramophone* and first-class opera encyclopaedias now list musicals under the heading of 'opera'. The public which flocks year after year to 'musicals' like *The Phantom of the Opera* or *Miss Saigon* has suddenly also taken the older art form to its heart.

Listening to an opera (or complete musical) on CD initially requires a degree of concentration. You can listen to a row of arias as a kind of better-class Muzak. You can do the same with a complete opera—but only after you have come to know it well, or if you have seen the work on stage. In most cases the latter is unlikely and, to gain the full benefit of continued as well as initial enjoyment from a substantial investment, the synopsis of the dramatic plot on which

Introduction

the music is built should be read first. It is desirable *at least once*, but not necessarily immediately, to listen to the full score while following the words in the libretto. The music has caused the whole thing to survive, but, as an entity, an opera is different from orchestral or symphonic music; the drama is created by the words being sung.

Composers of operas have always wanted the words to be understood by their audiences and before the 1950s most performances in all countries were given in the vernacular; the many recorded arias in languages other than the original proves this. Some knowledge of what is being sung is essential and only the full libretto can provide this. Opera houses now provide projected translated surtitles. The CD libretto does the same for you.

Consider this: musicals are always sung in the language of the audience. Would you enjoy *Miss Saigon* sung in Italian? If so, would you not want to read the libretto? The alternative, which this book also offers you, is a selection of highlights or arias. You don't have to work at listening to those—unless you start going to operas in the theatre. CDs of highlights alone are ideal in evaluating whether to pay the high prices which live performances of operas necessarily demand. And, if you like what you have seen on stage, complete CD sets will refresh your memory, in musically even better form, for years to come.

Can you get it?

The CDs in this book have been carefully chosen to be as up to date as possible. They include discs released in September 1995.

In my previous book, *The Good Classical CD Guide*, I made extensive comments about the availability, recording quality and the problems facing retailers as well as their customers where CDs are concerned. Short of reprinting all that here, even in reworded form, I will summarise what I said then.

Sound quality

Today's recording standards, in terms of sound, are so good that any disc made by a reputable manufacturer will satisfy the vast majority of people. This book is not intended for hi-fi buffs. All recordings listed are first-class technically. The importance of the performers (singers) is greater in opera than in symphonic music—many older recordings have been re-issued in CD form because the virtues of the performance far outweigh any minor shortcomings in sound quality.

I have used ADD and DDD to indicate the age of a recording; the year of production is really irrelevant to our enjoyment of a CD. ADD means that the recording was originally available on LP and was then transferred to CD; DDD means that it was made after the invention of the now standard type of disc. In opera, unlike symphonic music, the quality of the singers frequently outweighs the advantages of stereophonic sound, and many monaural and even original 78 rpm sets have been re-issued on CD. I have ignored pre-1950 sets in this book, but there are a number of 'mono' sets on which the vocal qualities outweigh any advantages of minimally better sound.

Availability

At the time of going to press, all recordings listed were on sale or obtainable through specialist record shops such as those recommended at the back of the book. However, the record trade is so volatile that changes in pricing, numbering and even labelling of individual recordings are taking place every month and anything which is not selling very well is often withdrawn from sale once stocks are exhausted. Even if this book were read on the very day of publication, one or two listed CDs could just have been deleted, but may still be available in some shops. More than one recording is listed wherever multiples exist and in the case of the most popular works, a maximum of three or four have been listed as the 'preferred' choices on the basis of my own knowledge and the recommendation of English, American and German major record reviewers. Occasionally there is one particular recording which is universally considered 'the best', but it may not include the buyer's favourite singers and there is no harm in choosing any of the alternatives offered.

Using this book

Abbreviations and symbols

★★★ very popular
★★ acceptable to most people
★ famous works unsuitable for newcomers to opera

A   pre-romantic opera, Mozart, baroque work, etc.
R   romantic work, 19th century
C   contemporary, 20th century opera
M   musical or operetta

d   dramatic
l   light
c   comic

CO   Chamber Orchestra
O   Orchestra
OC   Opera Company
PO   Philharmonic Orchestra
SO   Symphony Orchestra

ASMF   Academy of St Martin-in-the-Fields
BPO   Berlin Philharmonic Orchestra
CGO   Covent Garden Orchestra
ECO   English Chamber Orchestra
LPO   London Philharmonic Orchestra
LSO   London Symphony Orchestra
RPO   Royal Philharmonic Orchestra
VPO   Vienna Philharmonic Orchestra

$$$ full price
$$ mid or bargain price
$ super bargain

DDD   digital recording
ADD   analog recording, digitally remastered

s	soprano
ms	mezzo-soprano/contralto
t	tenor
ct	counter-tenor
b	baritone
ba	bass
c	conductor
ch	chorus
°	following the name of a composer or opera indicates that there is a more specific entry in the book

Works

Operas are listed in the text under the name of their composer. There is an alphabetical listing in the opera index at the back.

Titles

The original title of the opera is listed first, with (where applicable) an English translation in brackets. The most common translation is used; for example, you will find *The Marriage of Figaro* and not *Figaro's Wedding*, which is more correct, but only rarely used. English titles are used for operas in languages not using the standard alphabet, for example Russian.

Artists

The following order of artists is adopted throughout this book: singers, orchestra, conductor.

In the listing of casts in the text, the usual order has been adopted: soprano, mezzo-soprano, tenor, baritone, bass, except in those operas in which key roles do not follow this pattern; for example, in the case of *Carmen*, the mezzo-soprano (Carmen) precedes the soprano (Micaëla).

Choruses or choirs are not listed, as no opera CD set is likely to be bought on the strength of these often most valuable members of the cast.

Only the last names of artists are listed in the text. First names and voice types are included in the Index of Artists at the back.

Using this book

Arias

The most famous arias, duets and ensembles in each opera are listed before the commentary in order of popularity, not in the order in which they appear in the music. Each is followed by the type of singer (see Abbreviations and Symbols on page 13).

Acts

In many operas there is no consistent numbering of acts. Popular Verdi works, for example, exist in three/four or four/five act versions. Acts have only been listed to enable listeners to find the location of the famous set pieces in each work.

Plot outlines

For each opera there is a very brief synopsis of its story. Locations and periods have deliberately been omitted, because in recent years there has been a trend to change them from those the composer intended, even to modern or abstract settings. *Rigoletto*, supposedly located in Mantua in the sixteenth century, has been produced successfully as a modern Mafia morality play and a product of Mussolini's Italy. Music and words remain unchanged on CD, but prospective buyers could be misled if they attend a staging before purchase. Only the main story line is used; the many subplots are ignored.

Prices

The three price categories used are full, mid and bargain—approximately $30, $20 and $10. Prices and numbers and even labels (see below) are constantly being downgraded. No listed price should be higher than stated in this book. In the case of special imports (see below) it is almost impossible to find out what the retail price will be in Australia or New Zealand. All these have been marked as full price, but many, particularly highlights discs and operettas, may well be cheaper. I trust that no reader will object to paying less.

Record numbers

When prices are reduced (see above) record companies usually issue them with new numbers and, occasionally, under different labels. Thus a CD listed here which proves to be 'unobtainable' may well be in stock under a different number at a lower price and, when bargain-priced, even on a different label, for example, Decca, Philips and Deutsche Grammophon CDs of older vintage are sold as Belart discs.

Imports

The best record shops have CDs from UK, USA, Germany, France and other countries in stock and/or available to order and, if the latter, they can often be had in weeks rather than months. There is no such thing as one international catalogue listing everything which is obtainable. This book contains only recordings which any retailer can procure, though only a few specialist shops may be prepared to stock or import them all.

Please note: This book contains numerous CDs which are not listed in UK CD guides, particularly CDs of highlights from operas and operettas. Specialist shops in the UK are able to import discs from the Continent and the US, as can Australian and New Zealand shops, but their guides do not include these discs.

Credits

In establishing the most popular readily available CD sets in Australia, we gratefully acknowledge the help of Peter Posarnig, of Thomas' Record Shop in Melbourne.

WARNING

Do not buy multiple CD sets of operas on the basis of their fame or reputation alone. Some of the great masterpieces of the operatic repertoire are not readily accessible for the newcomer to the medium. Start with the works marked ★★★.

Using this book

SAMPLE ENTRY

1
MASSENET, Jules (1842–1912)   **3 4**
2 *Manon*   ★★ R d **5**

6 Cotrubas, Kraus, Quilico, Toulouse Capitole O, Plasson **7**
                                                              8
9 EMI CDS7 49610-2 (3 CDs) $$$ DDD **14**
                                        11

De los Angeles, Legay, Dens, Paris Opéra-Comique, Monteux (with Chausson: *Poème de l'amour et de la mer*)

10 EMI CMS7 63549 (mono) (3 CDs) $$ ADD **13**
                                            12

15
En fermant les yeux (The Dream) • Act 2 (t)
Ah! fuyez, douce image • Act 3 (t) **16**
Adieu, notre petite table • Act 2 (s)
Profitons bien de la jeunesse (Gavotte) • Act 3 (s)

17 A hundred years on, people are still mixing up Massenet's *Manon* with Puccini's *Manon Lescaut*° and sopranos are still **18** recording the 'Laughing Song' from Auber's *Manon Lescaut*. Massenet's . . .

The Plot The Chevalier des Grieux falls in love with innocent Manon and they set up house together. Manon is tempted by the good life and, when des Grieux is abducted by his father, she has no **19** problems finding richer lovers. The two meet again in a gaming hall in which both are arrested. Manon is to be deported and becomes seriously ill. Des Grieux tries to have her released, but she dies in his arms.

KEY

1	name of composer	**11**	full price
2	title of opera	**12**	mid or bargain price
3	acceptable to most people	**13**	analog recording, digitally remastered
4	romantic work, 19th century	**14**	digital recording
5	dramatic	**15**	best known arias
6	singers	**16**	singer type (in this case tenor, soprano)
7	orchestra	**17**	commentary
8	conductor	**18**	There is an entry for this work in this book
9	recording company		
10	record number	**19**	plot

17

Operas
ON CD

BEETHOVEN, Ludwig van (1770–1827)

Fidelio ★★ R d

Ludwig, Hallstein, Vickers, Berry, Frick, Philharmonia O, Klemperer
EMI CDS7 55170-2 (2 CDs) $$ ADD

Dernesch, Donath, Vickers, Kélémen, Ridderbusch, BPO, Karajan
EMI CMS7 69290-2 (2 CDs) $$ ADD
Highlights: **CDM7 63077-2 $$ ADD**

Norman, Coburn, Goldberg, Wlaschiha, Moll, Dresden Staatskapelle, Haitink
Philips 426 308-2 (2 CDs) $$$ DDD

Abscheulicher • *Act 1 (s)*
Mir ist so wunderbar • *Act 1 (s, s, t, ba)*
Gott, welch Dunkel hier • *Act 2 (t)*

While Beethoven is the most revered composer in history, he is not the most revered composer of operas. He wrote only one, rewrote it three times and ended up with a hybrid which, by any standards, is not what a good opera should be. Fortunately, it contains such a wealth of good music that it is impossible to ignore it, and the composer's republican sentiments ensure that its subject of freedom for all, which also dominates the finale of his ninth symphony, equates it with anti-totalitarianism. That made it a political tool during the days of the Cold War, but its musical highlights are enough to keep it in the regular repertoire. These are as much orchestral as vocal; Beethoven wrote four overtures to *Fidelio* and all are still being played regularly. The most famous is known as 'Leonora No. 3' and is frequently inserted in the second act.

The older recordings stand up well against the only digital one worth considering (Haitink), and that has a wonderful Leonora in Jessye Norman. On the other hand, in anything by Beethoven the conductor is vitally important, Klemperer and Karajan being the giants of the recent past. Jon Vickers is the Florestan of both; no present-day tenor is his equal.

Bellini

> **The Plot** Florestan is being held in a dungeon by the tyrannical Pizarro. His wife, Leonora, disguised as a man, Fidelio, gains employment with Rocco, who is in charge of Pizarro's many prisoners. Before the imminent arrival of a government minister, Pizarro tries to kill Florestan, but is foiled by Fidelio/Leonora, who saves her husband's life. The minister releases the prisoners and the opera ends in a hymn to liberty.

BELLINI, Vincenzo (1801–1835)

Norma ★★ R d

Sutherland, Horne, Alexander, Cross, LSO, Bonynge
Decca 425 488-2 (3 CDs) $$ ADD
Highlights: **Decca 436 303-2 $$ ADD**

Callas, Stignani, Fillipeschi, Rossi-Lemeni, La Scala Milan, Serafin
EMI CDS7 47304-2 (mono) (3 CDs) $$$ ADD
Highlights: **EMI CDM7 64419-2 $$ ADD**

Eaglen, Mei, La Scola, Kavrakos, Florence Maggio Musicale O, Muti
EMI CDS5 55471-2 (3 CDs) $$$ DDD

Casta diva • Act 1 (s)
Mira, o Norma • Act 2 (s & ms)
Ite sul colle • Act 1 (ba)

Norma is the operatic equivalent of *Hamlet* for sopranos. Every one of them wants to sing Norma, but very few can make a decent job of it. This is the epitome of what we call 'bel canto' operas. The phrase is really meaningless; it translates as 'beautiful song', but has become identified with the operas of Bellini, Rossini and Donizetti, which certainly must be sung beautifully—but so should Wagner! Norma differs from many other bel canto operas in that it requires not only a smooth flow of voice and the ability to decorate the music with clear and even elaborations, but a voluminous sound. Ideally Norma should be sung by a Tebaldi or Flagstad. For many years it lay unexplored with other works of the same genre, until Maria Callas and then Joan Sutherland suddenly gave it new life. Today *Norma* fills any opera house, if only to see whether the latest candidate is going to equal them.

Bellini

Norma is a starring vehicle for two great sopranos (the parts are interchangeable), but the tenor has little to do. Callas and Sutherland dominate the scene; both recorded the opera twice. In her second *Norma,* Sutherland had a more famous supporting cast (Caballé, Pavarotti, Ramey). But at fifty-eight the voice was no longer at its peak and Norma is the key character (Decca 414 476-2 $$$ DDD). The 1995 release, with Jane Eaglen as a fine Norma, returns to Bellini's original intentions by having a light soprano Adalgisa.

The Plot Gaul in pre-Christian times. Norma is in love with Pollione, a pro-consul of Rome, which occupies Gaul. They are not married, but have two children. Norma rails against the invaders, but Pollione, their leader, has fallen for the younger Adalgisa and threatens to take the children to Rome. She contemplates killing rather than losing them, but instead offers herself as a sacrifice to the gods to help her people, an act which re-ignites Pollione's love for her and they die together in the sacrificial fire.

I puritani ★★ R d

Sutherland, Pavarotti, Cappuccilli, Ghiaurov, CGO, Bonynge
Decca 417 588-2 (3 CDs) $$$ ADD

Caballé, Kraus, Manuguerra, Ferrin, Philharmonia O, Muti
EMI CMS7 69663-2 (2 CDs) $$ ADD

Callas, Di Stefano, Panerai, Rossi-Lemeni, La Scala Milan, Serafin
EMI CDS7 47308-2 (mono) (2 CDs) $$$ ADD

Qui la voce (Mad Scene) • Act 2 (s)
Son vergin vezzosa • Act 1 (s)
Suoni la tromba • Act 2 (b, ba)
Vieni fra queste braccia • Act 3 (t, s)
A te, o cara • Act 1 (t)

Bellini's answer to Donizetti's *Lucia di Lammermoor°*, except that *Puritani* was staged nine months before *Lucia*! Both make tremendous demands on the soprano, both have great Mad Scenes and both were forgotten until Callas and Sutherland brought them back to life. Elvira is possibly more difficult to sing than Lucia, but the opera does not have the dramatic impact of Donizetti's masterpiece. All the same, it has, if anything, even more good tunes which, when well sung, can bring an audience to its feet. Not only does Elvira have three Mad Scenes, to Lucia's one, but she ends the opera sane and in the arms of Arturo, whose impossibly difficult music takes him well above the top C; Bellini even asks for a top F at one point and some tenors actually do manage to sing this (in 'Vieni fra queste braccia')! *Puritani* is very much an opera for lovers of great singing, however weak its construction and ludicrous its story. Its failure to be heard more often is solely due to the fact that few sopranos, let alone tenors, are game to tackle it.

Of the three available recordings Sutherland's is easily the best and also the most complete. The extra money is well worth investing in this set.

| The Plot | The puritans of Plymouth (Scotland, according to Bellini!) are at war with the royalists. The action takes place in the castle of a Cromwell supporter in which the widow of the beheaded Charles I is hiding. She has little to sing, but is the key to the story. The royalist Arturo is betrothed to the puritan Elvira. Arturo helps the ex-queen to escape from the castle, leading Elvira to believe she has been deserted. She loses her mind. Arturo returns. She recovers. Arturo is sentenced to death. She loses her mind. The royalists are defeated and all traitors are pardoned. Elvira recovers. Happy end.

La sonnambula ★★ R d

Sutherland, Pavarotti, Ghiaurov, National PO, Bonynge
Decca 417 424-2 (2 CDs) $$$ DDD

Callas, Monti, Zaccaria, La Scala Milan, Votto
EMI CDS7 47378-8 (mono) (2 CDs) $$$ ADD

Ah, non credea mirarti • Act 3 (s)
Ah, non giunge • Act 3 (s)
Prendi, l'anel ti dono • Act 1 (t, s)
Vi ravviso • Act 1 (ba)

Like the other Bellini operas, *La sonnambula*, once forgotten, has recently made a remarkable comeback. The reason is probably that Bellini's tuneful music has come into fashion again and this opera has a starring role for the prima donna which relies on beauty of voice rather than spectacular coloratura displays. From 1831 until the turn of the century it was by far Bellini's most popular work, usually starring the most famous soprano of the time—Jenny Lind, Patti and the like. (For some reason Melba never sang Bellini at all.) *Sonnambula* is not, strictly speaking, a serious opera. Nor is it a comic one. A pastoral idyll probably describes it best. Yet, like most operas of its time, it also has a mad scene of sorts when Amina, the sonnambulist of the title, walks and talks (sings) in her sleep. The story line is straightforward and sensible. With the right cast it can be and is immensely successful.

Sutherland and Callas, as usual, share the vocal honours still unchallenged. Callas is better here than in *Puritani*°, but her recording is a late mono (1957) while Sutherland is early digital.

The Plot A village in Switzerland. Amina and Elvino are engaged to be married, but she has an unfortunate habit of walking in her sleep. When the lord of the manor stays overnight in the local inn, she blithely walks through his bedroom and across the rooftops quite oblivious to the fact that the rest of the villagers, and Elvino, naturally assume the worst. The delays in clearing up the mystery are designed to enable a whole lot of fine singing to take place.

BERNSTEIN, Leonard (1918–1990)

Candide ★★★ C I

(original cast) Cook, Petina, Rounseville, Adrian, O, Krachmalnick
Sony SK 48017 $$$ ADD

(intermediate version) Mills, Eisler, Langston, New York City Opera, Mauceri
New World NWCD 340/1 (2 CDs) $$$ DDD

(final version) Anderson, Ludwig, Hadley, Green, LSO, Bernstein
DG 429 734-2 (2 CDs) $$$ DDD

Glitter and be gay • Act 1 (s)
It must be so • Act 1 (t)
Eldorado • Act 2 (t)
What's the use? • Act 2 (s, t, ms, b)

Bernstein

Candide was pronounced dead many times before the death of its creator in 1990, but it won't lie down. At least fourteen different (very different) versions of it exist, including a 'definitive' one, which Bernstein himself recorded only months before his death. And that, let it be said, has already been decried by some. No doubt the Bernstein estate will insist on the last version at all times, but too many different recordings exist to say no to all the others. The reality is that Voltaire's curious morality tale about the best of all possible worlds has been transformed musically through a long series of excellent and most tuneful songs, arias, quartets and what have you, most with superb lyrics which have found a huge public. They are totally confusing and capable of many interpretations, but cannot be ignored and there is little doubt that *Candide* will survive, even though it will always have its critics. The overture alone must have been recorded hundreds of times by now.

The original cast is 'the' one everyone wants and it is superb, but who can argue with a composer's last thoughts?

The Plot The key figure in *Candide* is not the title role but the tutor/philosopher Pangloss, whose education of the innocent and simple youngster Candide is reflected in the adventures both have in the course of the opera. There is a huge variety of episodes of an almost abstract nature. Candide and the love of his life, Cunegonde, with Pangloss, experience everything which can be experienced, including death, which does not appear to be fatal! Candide travels the world, passing through a spell in a South American Eldorado, the Spanish inquisition, a Paris brothel, a casino in Venice—you name it, *Candide* has it. In the end they hope to 'build our house, and chop our wood, and make our garden grow'. After which Pangloss asks the audience: 'Any questions?'. Perhaps *Candide* is the best of all possible worlds.

Bernstein

West Side Story ★★★ M d

Te Kanawa, Troyanos, Horne, Carreras, Ollmann, O, Bernstein
DG 415 253-2 (2 CDs) $$$ DDD
Highlights: **DG 431 027-2 $$ DDD**

Nixon (for Natalie Wood), Wand (for Rita Moreno), Bryant, Chakaris, film soundtrack, J Green
Sony SK 48211 $$ ADD

Olafimihan, Manuel, Warnford, National SO, Edwards
TER TER2 1197 (2 CDs) $$$ DDD

Maria • Act 1 (s)
Tonight • Act 1 (t)
Somewhere • Act 2 (s)
I feel pretty • Act 2 (s)
America • Act 1 (ms)

West Side Story started as a musical and it is certainly musically light. Yet it is unquestionably dramatic, a modern version of *Romeo and Juliet* set in New York's Latin-American quarter—the West Side of the title. It broke new ground by having lengthy dance episodes, which are as important as its songs. They have found their way into the world's concert halls. We, therefore, have here a musically major work, even though many of its songs made the hit parades.

The film version closely approximates the Broadway original. Bernstein's complete recording with an all-star cast is magnificent, but more operatic than the score would seem to demand. The English cast treads an ideal middle path.

[The Plot] Tony and Maria belong to rival gangs of New York youths, the modern Montagues and Capulets. Tony accidentally kills Maria's brother in a gang fight. The messenger trying to deliver a note from Maria to Tony is so abused by his gang that she tells him Maria is dead. Tony allows himself to be killed in the next clash of violence. Unlike Juliet, Maria does not die, but points out the futility of the gang wars and expresses the hope of peace.

Bizet

BIZET, Georges (1838–1875)

Carmen ★★★ R d

De los Angeles, Micheau, Gedda, Blanc, French Radio O, Beecham
EMI CDC7 49240-2 (3 CDs) $$$ ADD

Baltsa, Ricciarelli, Carreras, Van Dam, BPO, Karajan
DG 410 088-2 (3 CDs) $$$ DDD
Highlights: **DG 413 322-2 $$$ DDD**

Troyanos, Te Kanawa, Domingo, Van Dam, LPO, Solti
Decca 414 489-2 (3 CDs) $$$ ADD
Highlights: **Decca 421 300-2 $$ ADD**

Highlights: Berganza, Domingo, Milnes, Cotrubas, LSO, Abbado
DG 439 496-2 $$ ADD

L'amour est un oiseau (Habanera) • *Act 1 (ms)*
La fleur que tu m'avais jetée (Flower Song) • *Act 2 (t)*
Votre toast (Toreador Song) • *Act 2 (b)*
Près des ramparts (Seguedilla) • *Act 1 (ms)*
Les tringles des sistres (Gypsy Song) • *Act 2 (ms)*
Je dis que rien ne m'épouvante • *Act 3 (s)*

Probably the most popular opera in the world today, *Carmen* was initially a failure and Bizet did not live to see its success. Nobody ever questions its excellence on any count today. The sordidness of its story was to blame for its original reception. Those who condemned it have been forgotten, but it may be noted that the music of *Carmen* so enchanted and inspired Tchaikovsky that his very next work, *Eugene Onegin*°, was a gigantic step forward compared with his earlier works.

For some reason *Carmen* is almost foolproof; even a bad performance can be enjoyed to an extent. It does not require great voices, but great artists, although the part of Don José is a stinker; he must be lyrically sweet in Act 1 and dramatically powerful at the end. Most tenors are at their best only early or late in the action. Carmen is a gypsy with violent emotions; the original story by Mérimée is a masterpiece of characterisation which leaves the door wide open to many different interpretations, tempting many a soprano to try her hand at a part which was a showpiece for contraltos at a time when contraltos,

Bizet

unlike today, were major box-office attractions; some of Carmen's music demands a strong lower register and there is not a top C in sight.

The best all-round set is probably the Karajan/Baltsa/Carreras, but what about the still miraculous Beecham, with the unlikely Victoria de los Angeles as an impressive, very unbitchy Carmen?! It surely beats the Decca recordings hands down on the strength of Beecham alone.

The Plot Carmen is arrested for fighting and the soldier José is ordered to take her to gaol. She bewitches him, is allowed to escape and José ends up in the lock-up instead. On release he joins Carmen and her gang of smugglers, but she falls for the toreador Escamillo. José goes away to see his dying mother and Carmen becomes Escamillo's girl. When she refuses the now half-demented José, he kills her. The character Micaëla does not exist in the original story, but every opera needs a soprano. The result: two messages from mum, one a beautiful duet in the first act and the other an aria in the third which invariably brings the house down.

Les pêcheurs de perles (The Pearl Fishers) ★★ R d

Alarie, Simoneau, Bianco, Lamoureux O, Fournet
Philips 434 782-2 (mono) (2 CDs) $$ ADD

Hendricks, Aler, Quilico, Capitole, Toulouse O, Plasson
EMI CDS7 49837-2 (2 CDs) $$$ DDD

Cotrubas, Vanzo, Sarabria, Paris Opéra O, Prêtre
CfP CFPD 4721 (2 CDs) $ ADD

Au fond du temple (In the depths of the temple) • Act 1 (t, b)
Je crois entendre • Act 2 (t)
Comme autrefois • Act 2 (s)

In his lifetime Bizet's most popular opera was *The Pearl Fishers*, because he died before *Carmen°* caught on. It was his first and last success, but not a lasting one. The opera disappeared almost completely until the recording of the duet 'In the depths of the temple' by Jussi Björling and Robert Merrill became a major hit just before the arrival of the long-playing record in 1950. Thereafter occasional revivals of this youthful imperfect work multiplied and today *The Pearl Fishers* is a regular repertoire piece. The reason lies solely in the wealth of great tunes, some repeated a little too often. The plot is ludicrous and structurally it is an immature work. The only way to describe it is 'pleasing'. It requires beautiful singing, of course, but there is nothing difficult about the music. Many a minor company with small voices has produced excellent versions and, theoretically, the recording microphone should have produced a whole stream of good CDs. Unfortunately it has not.

The 1953 mono Philips set is by far the best, in fact, the only totally satisfactory one musically. The EMI is acceptable, if that can be called a recommendation, and the bargain-priced Classics for Pleasure set, while better all around, uses the original score, which leaves the great tenor–baritone duet without a proper ending. Pity.

boxed(The Plot) The pearl fishers Nadir and Zurga are friends who both fell in love with the same woman many years ago. An unknown veiled virgin priestess, who has given up worldly love, arrives to stand vigil to ensure the safe return of the fishing fleet. Nadir discovers that she is the woman he and Zurga had loved. They meet secretly and renew their now forbidden love. Nadir and Leïla are arrested by Zurga, but he discovers that she saved his life many years ago and helps them to escape.

BOITO, Arrigo (1842–1918)

Mefistofele	★ R d

Ghiaurov, Freni, Caballé, Pavarotti, National PO, Fabritiis
Decca 410 175-2 (3 CDs) $$$ DDD
Prologue only: **Decca 440 922-2 $$ DDD**

Ramey, Marton, Domingo, Hungarian State O, Patanè
Sony S2K 44983 (2 CDs) $$$ DDD

Siepi, Tebaldi, Danieli, Del Monaco, St Cecilia Rome, Serafin
Decca 440 054-2 (2 CDs) $$ ADD

Dai campi, dai prati • Act 1 (t)
Giunto sul passo • Epilogue (t)
Son lo spirito • Act 1 (ba)
L'altra notte • Act 3 (s)
Lontano, lontano • Act 3 (s, t)

Boito

This is a remarkable work with some truly glorious music in it, but it is a sprawling collection of wonderful things which require great voices, and very few theatres ever have the courage to stage it. Among other things, it requires a great acting bass; the title role has been sung by Chaliapine, Christoff, Ghiaurov and the like. It is hardly known today, yet it is well worth investigating.

Arrigo Boito is famous today because he wrote the most perfect librettos ever produced by anyone for Verdi's *Otello*° and *Falstaff*°. He was a celebrated poet who wanted to be a composer. *Mefistofele* was the only opera he completed, if a work being constantly altered by its creator can be called completed. It is a great tragedy that the elusive art of producing a viable composite in the operatic genre eluded him, for Boito alone captured the true spirit of one of the world's greatest masterpieces, Goethe's *Faust*, on which so many other operas have been based. The whole of Gounod's *Faust*° is but a small part of Boito's epic recreation of Goethe in music. The man was a poet and a great thinker. If his compositional vein failed him—he left only one other, unfinished, opera—there are parts of *Mefistofele* (and I am not speaking of the arias above) which are positively sublime.

The Decca set starring Ghiaurov is obviously the one to have, unless you are a Domingo or Tebaldi fan.

The Plot In the Prologue Mefistofele (Mephisto) makes a wager with God that he can get Faust to sign over his soul to him in exchange for renewed life. To start, the opera parallels that of Gounod's *Faust*—the pact with the devil and the story of Margherita—but it includes a full-scale Walpurgisnight before she is found in prison for murdering her mother as well as her child. She dies defying Mephisto, though there is no ascent to heaven. Faust then meets Helen of Troy in ancient Greece. The Epilogue is pure Goethe. Faust longs to die, but Mephisto has not succeeded in causing him to say the equivalent of 'Stop the world, I want to get off', by which Mephisto wins his soul. It is Faust who is saved by angelic choirs, not Margherita.

THE
Basic Collection

Bizet	*Carmen*
Donizetti	*Don Pasquale*
Donizetti	*Lucia di Lammermoor*
Gounod	*Faust*
Leoncavallo	*Pagliacci*
Mascagni	*Cavalleria rusticana*
Mozart	*Don Giovanni*
Mozart	*The Magic Flute*
Mozart	*Nozze di Figaro*
Puccini	*Bohème*
Puccini	*Madama Butterfly*
Puccini	*Tosca*
Rossini	*Barber of Seville*
J Strauss	*Fledermaus*
Verdi	*Aida*
Verdi	*Rigoletto*
Verdi	*Traviata*
Verdi	*Trovatore*

CATALANI, Alfredo (1854–1893)

La Wally   R d

Tebaldi, Del Monaco, Cappuccilli, Monte Carlo Opera, Cleva
Decca 425 417-2 (2 CDs) $$ ADD

Marton, Araiza, Titus, Munich Radio O, Steinberg
BMG/Eurodisc RD 69073 (2 CDs) $$$ DDD

Ebben, ne andrò lontana • Act 1 (s)

This is not really a serious entry. In 1982 a French film, *Diva*, suddenly brought the above aria into the public domain and every soprano in sight is recording it. Catalani is a solitary figure who appeared in the midst of the new vogue for verismo, supposedly bringing real life into the artificial plots of old operas. Unfortunately, he died a year after Leoncavallo's *Pagliacci*° had solidly backed the movement started by Mascagni in *Cavalleria rusticana*°. *La Wally* (1892) actually preceded *Pagliacci* by three months and established Catalani as a serious contender on an ever-changing scene, but time ran out; he died at the age of only thirty-nine. Chances of seeing *La Wally* anywhere are just about nil, but it warrants inclusion here because of the huge demand for the aria.

|The Plot| Wally is driven from her home, because her father wants her to marry someone she does not love. On her father's death she inherits his money, but the man she loves, Hagenbach (the setting is the Tyrolean Alps), spurns her and she asks the originally rejected suitor to kill him. He attempts to do so, but Wally saves Hagenbach and they get together at last, only to be killed in an avalanche. Big deal!

CILEA, Francesco (1866–1950)

Adriana Lecouvreur ★★ R d

Scotto, Obraztsova, Domingo, Milnes, Philharmonia O, Levine
Sony M2K 79310 (2 CDs) $$ ADD

Sutherland, Ciurca, Bergonzi, Nucci, Welsh National Opera, Bonynge
Decca 425 815-2 (2 CDs) $$$ DDD

Tebaldi, Simionato, Del Monaco, Fioravanti, St Cecilia Rome, Capuana
Decca 430 256-2 (2 CDs) $$ ADD

Io sono l'umile ancella • Act 1 (s)
La dolcissima effigie • Act 1 (t)
L'anima ho stanca • Act 2 (t)
Poveri fiori • Act 4 (s)

Cilea was a major figure very briefly in the opera scene at the turn of the century. His *L'arlesiana* contains a tenor aria which is frequently recorded, but chances of a revival anywhere are not good. His one great success (which, incidentally, brought the young Caruso international fame) was *Adriana Lecouvreur*, based on the real life of a famous French actress of the early eighteenth century. Adriana is a wonderful part for any prima donna and many famous ones have insisted on its staging, thereby ensuring the continued existence of what is supposed to be box-office poison. There is no evidence that the combination of some wonderful tunes and four fine singers does not produce audiences, yet musical snobs love to dismiss the opera as worthless. If being tuneful and inoffensive is being worthless, so be it.

Sutherland and Bergonzi on a digital set should be ideal. They nearly are, yet both were in their late fifties when the set was made. Scotto is more convincing as a great actress. Adriana was Tebaldi's favourite role, but Del Monaco is on the rough side for Maurizio.

The Plot The actress Adriana is in love with Count Maurizio. The Princess de Bouillon wants Maurizio for herself. A bunch of violets given by Adriana to Maurizio is the key to the plot. At a private party the Princess makes advances to Maurizio, who foolishly gives her the violets. Arriving guests cause her to hide and Maurizio, with the help of Adriana, helps her to get away unnoticed. The ladies don't know each other, but the Princess recognises Adriana's voice and shows her the violets. Big scene of jealousy. Next day Adriana receives the violets by messenger. Believing them to be from Maurizio she smells them, inhaling the poison put on them by the Princess. Maurizio arrives. Great reunion. Adriana dies. Finis.

DÉLIBES, Léo (1836–1891)

Lakmé ★★ R d

Sutherland, Berbié, Vanzo, Bacquier, Monte Carlo Opera, Bonynge
Decca 425 485-2 (2 CDs) $$ ADD
Highlights: **Decca 436 305-2 $$ ADD**

Mesplé, Millet, Burles, Soyer, Opéra-Comique, Lombard
EMI CDS7 49430-2 (2 CDs) $$$ ADD
Highlights: **EMI CDM7 63447-2 $$ ADD**

Là-bas, dans la forêt (Bell Song) • Act 2 (s)
Viens, Mallika • Act 1 (s, ms)
Fantaisie aux divins mensonges • Act 1 (t)

Once one of the great showpieces for sopranos, *Lakmé* survives remarkably well, even though this kind of vehicle has gone out of fashion. The orientalism in plays and the visual arts of the late nineteenth century, combined with the undoubtedly melodious score, was bound to succeed. It is all very old-fashioned and the plot has some truly ridiculous aspects. The old dear is helped immensely by modern stage design, but there is not much point in staging *Lakmé* unless you have a Sutherland at your disposal. The famous 'Bell Song' used to be heard almost daily; today it has been supplanted by the barcarole 'Viens, Mallika' which, wrongly described as 'The Flower Duet', has invaded both television and films.

This is definitely a work which needs an outstanding soprano who has beauty of voice and easy coloratura delivery. Sutherland has both and Alain Vanzo is one of the finest tenors for this kind of music.

Mesplé has long been a favourite in Paris. If you hate Sutherland, by all means take Mesplé.

<u>The Plot</u> The India of the British Raj. Gerald, an English officer, falls in love with Lakmé, the daughter of a Brahmin priest. The father swears vengeance and, to identify the potential lover, makes Lakmé sing the 'Bell Song' in the market square. Gerald duly falls into the trap and is wounded in the melée which follows. Lakmé nurses him back to health, but when the bugle calls him back to duty he naturally leaves her for dead, which she compounds by smelling a poisonous flower.

DONIZETTI, Gaetano (1797–1848)

Don Pasquale ★★ R c

Mei, Lopardo, Allen, Bruson, Munich Radio O, R Abbado
BMG/RCA 09026 61924-2 (2 CDs) $$$ DDD

Freni, Winbergh, Nucci, Bruscantini, Philharmonia O, Muti
EMI CDS7 47068-2 (2 CDs) $$$ DDD
Highlights: **EMI CDC7 54490-2 $$$ DDD**

Hendricks, Canonici, Quilico, Bacquier, Lyon Opera, Ferro
Erato/Warner 2292-45487-2 (2 CDs) $$$ DDD

Quel guardo il cavaliere • Act 1 (s)
Com' è gentil (Serenade) • Act 3 (t)
Tornami a dir • Act 3 (s, t)
Cheti, cheti • Act 2 (b, ba)

*Q*uite possibly the best comic opera ever written, though not as famous as *The Barber of Seville*°. This is Donizetti's masterpiece, which is saying something for a composer who wrote no less than seventy-six operas, not counting many incomplete works. (*Don Pasquale* was No. 70!) The beauty of this comedy of manners is that its delightful music reflects some very touching human foibles, including the kind of genuine pathos which Walt Disney managed to avoid so carefully. A comedy which touches the heart strings. Think about it.

Incredibly, all three recommended sets are digitally recorded, though an old mid-price set which also includes Cimarosa's *Il maestro*

Donizetti

di capella sung by Fernando Corena and conducted by István Kertész (Decca 433 036-2, 2 CDs, $$ ADD) cannot be dismissed. Of the new sets, the latest has Renato Bruson still in his vocal prime, while both other Pasquales are past theirs, and Frank Lopardo is probably the best Ernesto. Still, all three have their merits.

The Plot Don Pasquale intends to disinherit his nephew because he has fallen in love with Norina, a widow. He consults Dr Malatesta as to the possibility of taking a wife himself to produce an heir. Malatesta is in cahoots with the nephew, Ernesto, and they play a rather nasty trick on the old man. Norina is passed off as Malatesta's sister, a very humble and retiring young lady. Once married, Norina becomes the worst kind of shrew and, worse, a spendthrift. Pasquale is embroiled in so many problems that he gladly annuls the marriage and allows the lovers to wed and have the inheritance.

L'elisir d'amore (The Elixir of Love)   ★★ R 1

Sutherland, Pavarotti, Cossa, Malas, ECO, Bonynge
Decca 414 461-2 (2 CDs) $$$ ADD

Devia, Alagna, Spagnoli, Praticò, ECO, Viotti
Erato/Warner 4509-91701-2 (2 CDs) $$$ DDD

Cotrubas, Domingo, G Evans, Wixell, CGO, Pritchard
Sony CD 79210 (2 CDs) $$ ADD

Highlights: Battle, Pavarotti, Nucci, Dara, Metropolitan O, Levine
DG 435 880-2 $$$ DDD

Una furtiva lagrima • Act 2 (t)
Quanto è bella • Act 1 (t)
Venti scudi • Act 2 (t, b)
Udite, udite • Act 1 (ba)

Although *L'elisir d'amore* does not have as many famous set pieces as *Don Pasquale*°, it gets as many productions, or more, world-wide. No doubt 'Una furtiva lagrima' has something to do with it, but nobody is likely to be disappointed in the rest of the music. Apart from Dulcamara's patter song, there is nothing difficult about it, no screaming top Cs to frighten the horses and the comedy is delicious. *Elisir* also happens to be the ideal vehicle for any good tenor who can't act; he is supposed to be a bit of a simpleton and if he just stands around looking dumb, as many tenors do in all their parts, it matters not at all. Not that that would mean anything to CD buyers, who will get all the humour they need from the music and the libretto, which is certainly essential for any recorded comedy.

Sutherland/Pavarotti are hard to beat, but Alagna, a coming tenor star, sings 'Una furtiva lagrima' better than Domingo and Cotrubas is probably the best Adina of them all.

|The Plot| Nemorino is a simple soul who has taken the story of Tristan and Isolde and their love potion as fact. He loves Adina and is taken in by the quack doctor Dulcamara, who peddles cheap wine, claiming that anyone who drinks it will become attractive to the one whose love is sought. Adina playfully flirts with the army sergeant Belcore. Nemorino is desolate; he does not have enough money to buy another dose of the false elixir, so enrols in the army to gain the twenty ducats enrolment fee and starts on his second bottle while crying over Adina's infidelity ('Una furtiva lagrima'). Village rumour has it that Nemorino has inherited a lot of money and all the village girls are suddenly fawning on him. The elixir is working, thinks Nemorino. But Adina really loves him and has bought his freedom from Belcore. They get together without either knowing or caring whether the inheritance is real.

La Fille du régiment (The Daughter of the Regiment) ★★ R1

Sutherland, Pavarotti, Malas, CGO, Bonynge
Decca 414 520-2 (2 CDs) $$$ ADD

Pour mon âme • Act 1 (t)
Il faut partir • Act 1 (s)
Salut à la France • Act 2 (s)

The Daughter of the Regiment came back to life through Joan Sutherland's unlikely success in it at Covent Garden in 1966 and elsewhere for many years. Its original popularity, which continued until the days of Lily Pons in the thirties, was due totally to pretty girls with tiny voices twittering sweetly. Sutherland hardly fitted that description, but clowned it up with such élan (backed by Luciano Pavarotti) that the *Daughter*'s virtues have suddenly been rediscovered. The critics no longer pan it and every young tenor wants to have a go at the nine top Cs in one minute (not very hard)

Donizetti

which 'Pour mon âme' demands, but none of the arias is 'popular' in the normal sense of the word, because few recordings of them were best-sellers in the days of 78s. This is the lightest of Donizetti, and certainly not a masterpiece. It is about as close to a musical or Broadway show as anything in the operatic repertoire.

Only one studio recording of it exists on CD, but that is a beauty in every respect. A live recording in 1989 on the Nuova Era label is not in the same street. But the opera is a delight.

The Plot Marie is a foundling who has been brought up by the soldiers of a French regiment and is now their lucky mascot. Tonio wants to marry her, but the 'fathers' of the regiment insist that she can only marry one of their own. So Tonio enlists and the engagement is on. But not for long. The Marquise de Birkenfeld insists that she is Marie's aunt and that the girl must take up her rightful place in society; the army is not for one of her exalted family. Tonio has to stay with the regiment, which turns Tonio into a war hero. The Marquise admits that the girl is actually her own daughter and gives her blessing to their union.

Lucia di Lammermoor ★★★ R d

Sutherland, Pavarotti, Milnes, Ghiaurov, CGO, Bonynge
Decca 410 193-2 (2 CDs) $$$ ADD
Highlights: **Decca 421 885-2 $$ ADD**

Callas, Di Stefano, Gobbi, Arié, Maggio Musicale Fiorentino O, Serafin
EMI CMS7 69980-2 (mono) (2 CDs) $$ ADD
Highlights: **EMI CDM7 64420-2 (mono) $$ ADD**

Studer, Domingo, Pons, Ramey, LSO, Marin
DG 435 309-2 (2 CDs) $$$ DDD

Highlights: Gruberová, Shicoff, Agache, LSO, Bonynge
Teldec 4509-93692-2 $$$ DDD

Ardon gl'incensi • *Spargi d'amaro (Mad Scene)* • *Act 2 (s)*
Chi mi frena • *Act 2 (sextet)*
Fra poco a me recovero • *Act 2 (t)*
Regnava nel silenzio • *Act 1 (s)*
Verrano a te • *Act 1 (s, t)*

Donizetti

Incredible as it may seem today, this most popular of all bel canto operas also had its years of obscurity, which were ended by the appearance of Maria Callas and, subsequently, Joan Sutherland. Donizetti's comic operas have always been in the spotlight, yet he wrote vastly more serious works than comic ones and this is the best of them all. It exemplifies the early romantic period to perfection, even to being based on a novel by Sir Walter Scott, *The Bride of Lammermoor*. Scott was incredibly popular all over Europe. About eighty operas used his books as a source and Scotland was considered the ideal location for any opera plot (see Bellini's *Puritani°*). Every major coloratura soprano since 1835 has sung Lucia, whose music is so singable that even tiny little voices have had sensational successes in it. There is certainly no lack of Lucias today. Her fame is so great that few people consider the fact that the tenor's part is almost as big as Lucia's; in fact, he has the whole final scene to himself—*after* Lucia's Mad Scene, which has fooled more than one patron into leaving the theatre under the impression that it is all over. It is not, and it takes a good tenor to follow that most famous of all soprano arias, but Donizetti gives him some superb music to end the opera.

Callas and Sutherland again set the standard, but the remarkable Cheryl Studer has produced an acceptable digital alternative, with Domingo amazingly good in strange territory for him. Callas recorded *Lucia* three times and all three are still in the same company's catalogue! All are monaural and I have chosen the earliest as being the best. Sutherland's is her second recording, not quite as good as her first, which is also still available—Renato Cioni is no Pavarotti, even though Robert Merrill and Cesare Siepi are first-class (Decca 411 622-2, 2 CDs, $$ ADD).

| The Plot | Lucia is in love with Edgardo, much to the disgust of her brother Enrico. While Edgardo is in France to help the Stuarts regain the throne, Enrico forges a letter proving him to have been unfaithful. He presses Lucia to marry Arturo, thereby saving his own political skin. Lucia agrees to the marriage, but as she signs the wedding contract Edgardo returns and is faced with Lucia being wed to another. His anger and Lucia's desperation lead to her murder of Arturo, her insanity and death. Edgardo kills himself.

DVOŘÁK, Antonín (1841–1904)

Rusalka ★★ R d

Beňačková, Soukupová, Ochman, Novák, Czech PO, Neumann
Supraphon 10 3641-2 (3 CDs) $$$ DDD
Highlights: **Supraphon 1122522 $$$ DDD**

O silver moon • Act 1 (s)

Only one aria keeps *Rusalka* in the eyes of the general public, yet the score is full of beautiful music—just try the great love duet which is sung by the tenor alone! (See plot below.) Dvořák wrote ten operas, all of which can be heard still in what are now separate states, the Czech Republic and Slovakia. Elsewhere only *Rusalka* has found a permanent niche and that only recently; the Metropolitan gave it its first showing there as late as 1993 and Covent Garden has not yet come around to it. Yet this is a continuously tuneful score without a dull moment, perhaps a little sugary here and there, but *Rusalka* is a fairy tale without any great dramatic punches; how else do you portray a heroine unable to speak, let alone sing, for a major part of the action?

The only CD recording is, happily, superb in every way. Beňačková is unchallenged by past or present protagonists in the title role.

The Plot Rusalka is a water sprite who falls in love with a human Prince. She may leave her watery home to join him, but as a mortal woman she loses her voice. The Prince soon grows tired of his silent bride, takes up with a foreign princess and Rusalka returns to her lake. Now able to speak again, she warns the repentant Prince that he cannot have her back; if she kisses him, he will die. He accepts the fatal kiss and she resumes her subaquatic existence.

FLOTOW, Friedrich von (1812–1883)

Martha ★★ R1

Popp, Soffel, Jerusalem, Ridderbusch, Bavarian Radio O, Wallberg
Eurodisc 352 878 (2 CDs) $$ ADD

Rothenberger, Fassbaender, Gedda, Prey, Bavarian State Opera, Heger
EMI CMS7 69339-2 (2 CDs) $$ ADD

Berger, Ruziczka, Anders, Greindl, Berlin Staatskapelle, Schüler
Berlin 002 1632 (2 CDs) $$ ADD

Ach, so fromm (M'appari) • Act 3 (t)
Die letzte Rose (The Last Rose of Summer) • Act 2 (s)
Gute Nacht (Good Night) • Act 2 (t, s, b, ms)
Mag der Himmel euch vergeben • Act 3 (t, s, b, ms)
Lasst mich euch fragen (Porter Song) • Act 3 (ba)

At the turn of the century *Martha* was usually performed in English-speaking countries in Italian and in that language it was a staple diet at the Metropolitan and Covent Garden. And why not, when its production was demanded by tenors like Caruso and Gigli, to give them a chance to be heard in their best-selling recording of 'M'appari'? Although German tenors sang 'Ach, so fromm', tenors in the pre-World War II period had to be Italian and none so born failed to record it. You could also buy it in French, Russian, Hungarian or Czech, but there is no recording in English of 'Like a dream' from that famous German opera set in Richmond, England. Even in post-war years Richard Tucker and Jussi Björling were recording 'M'appari', which was as big a hit as 'Nessun dorma' for a hundred years before Pavarotti's favourite aria pushed it from its perch. (Domingo and Pavarotti have, of course, recorded this 'Italian' aria as well.)

Why *Martha* has not followed in the footsteps of the many once-forgotten, now-restored Italian operas is a bit of a mystery. There have always been complete recordings of it, the score is melodious

Flotow

throughout and the plot almost makes sense by operatic standards, although the famous aria is really part of a Mad Scene—for the tenor! The trend to sing operas in the original language has probably killed off this delightful work. It always was a tenor star vehicle outside Germany and no Italian or Spaniard will sing it in German today. Its neglect everywhere but on CD is truly incomprehensible. *Martha* is a much better work than many operas in the standard repertoire.

Every one of the above recordings is first-class, but the wonderful Berlin performance was made in 1944!

The Plot Lady Harriet and her maid go to the Fair at Richmond and, as a lark, allow themselves to be hired as servants by two farmers. The joke backfires, because the contract binds them legally for a year. They have to steal away during the night. Farmer Lionel goes out of his mind when his 'Martha' is missing, even though it is discovered that he is the lost heir of Lord Derby. To snap him out of his mental disturbance, Harriet and Nancy restage the Fair at Richmond, complete with hiring booth, and both marry their ex-employers.

THE TOP TEN
Sopranos in Operas
ON CD

Montserrat CABALLÉ
Maria CALLAS
Victoria DE LOS ANGELES
Mirella FRENI
Edita GRUBEROVÁ
Elisabeth SCHWARZKOPF
Cheryl STUDER
Joan SUTHERLAND
Renata TEBALDI
Kiri TE KANAWA

GERSHWIN, George (1898–1937)

Porgy and Bess ★★ C d

Haymon, Blackwell, White, Glyndebourne, LPO, Rattle
CDS7 49568-2 (3 CDs) $$$ DDD
Highlights: **EMI CDC7 54325-2 $$$ DDD**

L Mitchell, Hendricks, White, Cleveland O, Maazel
Decca 414 559-2 (3 CDs) $$$ ADD

Dale, Lane, Albert, Houston Grand Opera, DeMain
BMG/RCA RD 82109 (3 CDs) $$$ ADD
Highlights: **BMG/RCA RD 84680 $$$ ADD**

Highlights: L Price, Warfield, RCA Victor O, Henderson
BMG/RCA GD 82046 $$$ ADD

Summertime • Act 1 (s)
Bess, you is my woman now • Act 2 (s, b)
I got plenty o' nuttin' • Act 1 (b)
It ain't necessarily so • Act 2 (t)

A flop on Broadway, where it was staged as an 'American folk opera' in 1935, *Porgy and Bess* emerged as a major musical in 1952, when a world tour of a new production ran for three and a half years. It set out as a musical and returned as an opera. Its original cast was headed by Leontyne Price and William Warfield, unknown black singers at a time when negroes were still banned from the stage of the Metropolitan—which wanted to stage the original in 1935 with white singers in black-face, something Gershwin refused. Still, the first recordings of extracts were made by Lawrence Tibbett and Helen Jepson—of the Metropolitan! That original touring company even gave seven performances at La Scala in Milan. That was some musical! Since then *Porgy and Bess* has been seen in full operatic productions in every major city of the world, though few opera companies can tackle an all-negro opera; even the Metropolitan only managed sixteen performances—in 1985!

Gershwin

Porgy is not only the first American opera to become world-famous, but the first to use jazz seriously instead of satirically. In spite of some humorous arias and the jazz element, this is a very dramatic work with elaborate ensembles and a lot of chorus work echoing negro spirituals by a composer better known in the field of popular song. The original drama on which it was based was an attack on racial prejudice and the tragic story is vastly superior to those of most operas. Beautiful as it is, it is not an opera for starters.

Surprisingly enough, the Glyndebourne production of 1992 is by far the best performance and recording ever made.

| The Plot | Bess is the woman of the stevedore Crown, who kills a man and flees, leaving Bess destitute. The cripple Porgy takes her in and shelters her. Crown returns and brutally beats her. Porgy nurses her back to health, but later kills Crown in a fair fight and is taken for interrogation by the police. A smart cookie, Sporting Life, tells Bess that Porgy will not return. She goes with him to New York. When Porgy is released, because no witnesses to the killing are prepared to give evidence, he finds Bess gone and leaves for the big city to find her. There are numerous subplots and some of the arias, including 'Summertime', are not even sung by the protagonists of the title.

GIORDANO, Umberto (1867–1948)

Andrea Chénier ★★★ R d

Scotto, Domingo, Milnes, National PO, Levine
RCA GD 82046 (2 CDs) $$ ADD

Caballé, Pavarotti, Nucci, National PO, Chailly
Decca 410 117-2 (2 CDs) $$$ DDD

Tebaldi, Del Monaco, Bastianini, St Cecilia Rome, Gavazzeni
Decca 425 407-2 (2 CDs) $$ ADD

Un dì all'azzurro (Improvviso) • *Act 1 (t)*
Come un bel dì di maggio • *Act 4 (t)*
La mamma morta • *Act 3 (s)*
Nemico della patria • *Act 3 (b)*
Sì, fui soldato • *Act 3 (t)*
Vicino a te • *Act 4 (t, s)*

Giordano

Umberto Giordano is not exactly the world's most famous composer, but his *Andrea Chénier* has held the stage surprisingly well, mainly because it has one of opera's most rewarding tenor roles—it is reasonably static and has no less than three major arias and a duet in which show-offs can show off spectacularly. Opportunities for sweetness of tone also abound; Chénier is a poet after all. It used to be Gigli's favourite opera and has been recorded by just about every major tenor star. There are also fine arias for the soprano and the baritone, which have been recorded individually by all the great singers of the century. *Chénier* has as many beautiful set pieces as any other opera, though they may not be as famous as those by Puccini or Verdi. No wonder the opera holds the stage, though it belongs to the blood-and-thunder variety—but so does *Tosca*°. Of subtlety there is very little, but for full-blooded singing it is hard to beat. André Chénier was a real-life person, a poet who took part in the French Revolution and was one of the last to go to the guillotine. The opera is historically correct, though the inevitable love affair is fictional; it was invented by the librettist Luigi Illica and almost exactly parallels the plot of *Tosca*, co-written by the same Illica for Puccini four years later.

Your preference in tenors will determine which set to buy. Del Monaco/Tebaldi are ideal belters, Domingo/Scotto the most poetic and Pavarotti/Caballé the most expensive—because it is a DDD recording; not the most important thing in this field, except perhaps in the non-sung crashing finale.

> **The Plot** Andrea Chénier is a guest in the home of Maddalena, where Gerard is one of the servants; he becomes a leading figure of the revolution in Act 2. Chénier and Gerard are friends, but rivals for the hand of Maddalena, now an ex-aristocrat. When Chénier is arrested, Gerard agrees to drop the charge of treason against his ex-friend if she will give herself to him, but he is sentenced to death by the court in spite of Gerard's attempted exoneration. Maddalena decides to go to the guillotine with Chénier. And they all died happily ever after.

Gluck

GLUCK, Christoph Willibald von (1714–1787)

Orfeo ed Euridice (Orphée) ★★ A d

Argenta, Chance, Beckerbauer, Stuttgart Tafelmusik, Bernius
Sony SX2K 48040 (2 CDs) $$$ DDD

Hendricks, Von Otter, Fournier, Lyon Opera, Gardiner
EMI CDS7 49834-2 (2 CDs) $$$ DDD

Speiser, Baker, Gale, LPO, Leppard
Erato/Warner 2292-45864-2 (2 CDs) $$ DDD
Highlights: **Erato/Warner 4509985122 $$ DDD**

Highlights: Ayars, Ferrier, Vlachopoulos, Southern PO, Stiedry
Decca 433 468-2 $$ ADD

Che farò senza Euridice • *Act 3 (ms or ct)*
Che puro ciel • *Act 2 (ms or ct)*

Gluck was the father of operatic drama as we know it; he was the first to adapt the music to the meaning of the words being sung and *Orfeo* is the history-making example of his innovations. The story has been set by umpteen other composers from the accepted first opera ever, on the same subject, by Jacopo Peri in 1600, to a 1986 version by Harrison Birtwhistle. Gluck's is by far the most popular one, though it is difficult (in fact, impossible) to reconstruct the original, since the first Orpheus was a castrato. Gluck himself rewrote the part for a tenor for Paris in 1774 and added a lot of very fine music. The French version has yet to appear on CD. It introduced the major ballet scenes which now form some of the most popular parts of the score; sometimes they are even included in so-called 'original' versions in Italian! Until fairly recently Orpheus was always sung by a contralto, in a rearrangement made by Berlioz in 1859. The new vogue for counter-tenors has brought the part back into the male domain, but CD sets use either alternative.

The Sony has not only the advantage of a beautiful counter-tenor as Orpheus, but a treble in the part of Amor, avoiding any confusion between the semi-god and Euridice. EMI uses the Berlioz version with three very fine soloists and the Erato features Dame Janet Baker's last appearance on stage in the 1982 Glyndebourne production. Her colleagues are not as good, but Raymond Leppard conducts a classic production built around Baker's superlative Orpheus. And it is at mid-price!

The Plot Euridice having died, Orpheus tries to retrieve her from the nether world with the help of Amor, the God of Love. The beauty of his singing overcomes the Furies barring his way, but Amor has imposed a difficult condition on his rescue mission: Orpheus must not look back at Euridice, who is following. She is distressed by his apparent indifference and he does turn around, only to see her die again. Amor relents and the couple are reunited.

GOUNOD, Charles (1818–1893)

Faust ★★★ R d

Gasdia, Hadley, Agache, Ramey, Welsh National O, Rizzi
Teldec 4509-90872-2 (3 CDs) $$$ DDD

Studer, Leech, Hampson, Van Dam, Toulouse Capitole O, Plasson
EMI CDS7 54228-2 (3 CDs) $$$ DDD
Highlights: **EMI 754 358-2-567**

De los Angeles, Gedda, Blanc, Christoff, Paris Opéra, Cluytens
EMI CMS7 69983-2 (3 CDs) $$ ADD

Highlights: Freni, Domingo, Ghiaurov, Allen, Paris Opéra, Prêtre
EMI CDM7 63090-2 $$ ADD

Highlights: Sutherland, Corelli, Ghiaurov, LSO, Bonynge
Decca 421 861-2 $$ ADD

Salut! demeure chaste et pure • Act 3 (t)
Air des bijoux (Jewel Song) • Act 3 (s)
Le veau d'or (Calf of Gold) • Act 2 (ba)
Even bravest hearts (Avant de quitter) • Act 2 (b)
Soldiers' Chorus • Act 4 (ch)
Il se fait tard (Love Duet) • Act 3 (t, s)
Mephisto's Serenade • Act 4 (ba)

This is the opera with which the Metropolitan Opera House opened its doors in 1883 and then played it so frequently that it became known as the 'Faustspielhouse', a pun on Bayreuth's Festspielhaus. At the turn of the century *Faust* was undoubtedly by far the most popular opera in the world and its universal favour only waned after World War II. At the moment it is suddenly emerging

Gounod

with renewed strength, which is not surprising when you consider the number of famous arias from it which have been recorded over the years.

Gounod only deals with one short episode of Goethe's *Faust*, which is to Germany what *Hamlet* is to England. The dramatic sequence is simple and logical, but padded rather heavily with arias and even long scenes which once upon a time were usually cut. Today *Faust* is recorded in full, making three CDs essential. Most of the formerly cut music is far from inspiring, but the highlights are indeed high lights. Valentin's aria was added for the original London production, which was sung in English. Strictly speaking, any 'original' score should have him singing 'Even bravest hearts may swell', but that would be, and is, ridiculous. Yet, oddly enough, it can be heard in that language on CD. In 1929 Sir Thomas Beecham recorded *Faust* in English with Heddle Nash and Miriam Licette and that excellent performance was issued on CD in 1994 (Dutton Laboratories 2CDAX 2001, 2 CDs) with the Australian Harold Williams singing the original words of that aria. Vocally and orchestrally that old recording has the edge on some of the listed CDs, but it is not for the average collector.

For once, the most recent set from Teldec outpaces all previous ones, though the singers do not include any great stars (yet?). It is by far the most satisfactory recording made to date, but Studer and Van Dam are fine on another modern recording, while the old Cluytens set (more than an hour shorter than the other two) has Boris Christoff as a magnificent Mephisto and Victoria de los Angeles as a delightful Marguerite.

The Plot The aging philosopher Faust makes a pact with Mephisto, pledging his soul in return for his youth and unlimited wealth. In his second youth-hood he seduces the innocent Marguerite, with the help of Mephisto. She loses her reason when her brother Valentin dies in a duel with Faust and kills their child. In her prison cell Mephisto bargains with Heaven for her soul, but is denied. She ascends, while Faust descends to you-know-where.

Gounod

Roméo et Juliette (Romeo and Juliet) ★★ R d

Malfitano, Kraus, Quilico, Van Dam, Toulouse Capitole O, Plasson
EMI CDS7 47365-8 (3 CDs) $$$ DDD

Micheau, Jobin, Mollet, Rehfuss, Paris Opéra, Erede
Decca 443 539-2 (2 CDs) $$ ADD

Freni, Corelli, Depraz, Gui, Paris Opéra, Lombard
EMI CMS5 65290-2 (2 CDs) $$ ADD

Je veux vivre (Waltz Song) • Act 1 (s)
Ah, lève-toi, soleil • Act 2 (t)
Nuit d'hyménée • Act 4 (t, s)
Ange adorable • Act 1 (t, s)

In Melba's day, Gounod's *Romeo and Juliet* was a top attraction. For some years, with Melba and Jean de Reszke in the leads, it was even more popular than *Faust* in Paris, London and New York. Time has not dealt kindly with this opera. It must be admitted that it is a poor setting of Shakespeare's great play. However, the music is invariably tuneful and with good singers and a fine production it now features regularly as part of the world-wide opera explosion of recent years. The famous 'Waltz Song' is a musical anachronism, even though it remains the most often-heard extract. It was added during rehearsals on command of the opera director's wife, who was the original Juliet and did not want to sing the dramatic aria Gounod had written for the last act; there was no coloratura in it! The rest of the opera is lyrically suitable for the subject and has nothing to do with the vocal brilliance of this aria.

For many years the only CD set available was the ancient and far from good Decca recording, the only merit of which is its cheapness and the fact that it includes the usually omitted ballet music. The 1985 DDD set, deleted in England but available here, has Alfredo Kraus' aging Romeo, still superior to many a younger tenor, and a fine supporting cast. Freni/Corelli provide star singing, but are hardly idiomatic.

The Plot Romeo and Juliet are lovers belonging to rival families and are secretly married. When, in the course of a duel Romeo kills Juliet's brother, the fat is in the fire. To avoid a forced marriage to another, Juliet is given a sleeping potion which leaves her apparently dead. The news of the ruse does not reach Romeo who, believing Juliet has really died, takes poison. When she wakes and finds his body, she kills herself. (As if you didn't know!)

HALÉVY, Fromental (1799–1862)

La Juive (The Jewess) ★ R d

Varady, Anderson, Carreras, González, Furlanetto, Philharmonia O, Almeida
Philips 420 190-2 (3 CDs) $$$ DDD

Rachel, quand du Seigneur • Act 4 (t)
Si la rigeur • Act 1 (ba)
O Dieu de nos pères (Passover Scene) • Act 3 (t, ch)

Rarely heard these days, *La Juive* is one of the grandest of the French grand operas, demanding huge productions and great singers. The fact that the only recording of it is far from flawless points up the difficulties facing its survival, which ought to be assured on musical grounds. Even the over-dramatic plot is not as silly as those of many more famous works. It is, in fact, most relevant in our time of racial hatreds; anti-semitism was the cause of the Holocaust and both score and music should appeal to the Jewish community; there is even a Passover celebration in the second act. The central role is curious in that it features the leading tenor as the father, while a secondary tenor provides the love interest. Eléazar was Caruso's last and greatest part and Carreras does not have a Caruso-sized voice. Julia Varady, on the other hand, is outstanding in the title role and June Anderson contrasts nicely with her as the Princess Eudoxie.

The Plot Rachel, the daughter of Eléazar, the Jewish goldsmith, is in love with Prince Léopold, who is in disguise. When she discovers that he is a Christian and married, she admits publicly that he has seduced a Jewess—herself. Cardinal Brogni sentences Léopold, Rachel and

Eléazar to death. Rachel, out of love for Léopold, manages to save him. She and her father are offered a pardon if they will renounce Judaism. They refuse and go to their death. Rachel, of course, turns out to have been the Cardinal's long-lost daughter.

HANDEL, George Frideric (1685–1759)

Alcina ★ A d

Sutherland, Sinclair, Berganza, Alva, Sciutti, Freni, Flagello, LSO, Bonynge (with *Julius Caesar°* highlights)
Decca 433 723-2 (3 CDs) $$ ADD

Augér, D Jones, Kuhlmann, Harrhy, Kwella, M Davies, Tomlinson, London Baroque Sinfonia, Hickox
EMI CDS7 49771-2 (3 CDs) $$$ DDD

Handel's operas contain a wealth of fine music which can be enjoyed by all, but in their complete form a degree of monotony sets in. Aria follows aria follows aria; *Alcina* has but a single ensemble and that is the finale. On stage this fault can be, and has been, successfully hidden by visual action. On disc these works will appeal only to the aficionado because of their length. Nevertheless, some must be included here and *Alcina* is probably the most tuneful of them all; not forgetting that it has some delightful extended ballets, though not a single aria which is universally famous.

The re-issue of the 1962 recording is clearly prompted by the attraction of Joan Sutherland. Without her the public stayed away from complete Handel on disc. The fact that this version is abridged may well make it more attractive to the prospective buyer, particularly because it has a filler of highlights from *Julius Caesar°* sung by Sutherland, Marilyn Horne and Margreta Elkins. The EMI Hickox version is absolutely complete, absolutely the best sound, absolutely the best sung and absolutely the most expensive.

The Plot Alcina is a sorceress who holds Ruggiero prisoner on her island. Ruggiero's affianced, Bradamante, arrives disguised as her own brother Ricciardo in an attempt to rescue him. Alcina customarily discards her lovers and then turns them into beasts. Alcina fancies 'Ricciardo' as her next, but Bradamante manages to free Ruggiero

Handel

from her power and, by means of a magic ring, returns all of Alcina's beasts to human form.

Giulio Cesare *(Julius Caesar)* ★ A d

Larmore, Schlick, Fink, Rørholm, Ragin, Zanasi, Concerto Köln, Jacobs
Harmonia Mundi HMC 901385/7 (3 CDs) $$$ DDD

(in English) Baker, Masterson, Walker, D Jones, Bowman, Tomlinson, English National Opera, Mackerras
EMI CMS7 69760-2 (3 CDs) $$ DDD
Highlights: **EMI CDM7 63724-2 $$ DDD**

Highlights: Pushee, Kenny, Campbell, Gunn, Dalton, Australian Opera, Hickox
ABC 446 271-2 $$$ DDD

Piangerò, la sorte mia • Act 3 (s)
Va tacito e nascosto • Act 1 (ms or ct)

Due to the recent outstanding production of *Julius Caesar* by the Australian Opera this work will be of greater interest to local Handel buyers than most, and it is a worthy contender, although there have been so many different ways of presenting this monumentally long work that the endless arias, none of which can be said to be famous on its own merits, can be bought as sung by contraltos, counter-tenors and even baritones.

The above recommendations include two kinds of Caesar; two mezzo-sopranos, Janet Baker and the magnificent Jennifer Larmore (fast approaching the status of the next Marilyn Horne); and an excellent counter-tenor, Graham Pushee. The complete opera on Harmonia Mundi includes a free fourth CD, while the fine version in English fits everything on three and is medium priced. Its excellent cast is headed by Janet Baker. The highlights disc is probably the best buy for the novice in this field; it is a pity that this superb Australian performance was not released in more complete form.

The Plot Cleopatra introduces herself to Caesar in disguise, but when he keeps his assignation with 'Lidia' he is told that he has been betrayed and is to be killed by the approaching Egyptians. Cleopatra, as Queen of Egypt, convinces him to flee. The Romans conquer

Egypt and imprison Cleopatra, but Caesar has escaped injury and restores the throne, though not the country, to Cleopatra.

Semele ★ A c

Battle, Horne, Aler, Chance, Ramey, English Chamber O, Nelson
DG 435 782-2 (3 CDs) $$$ DDD

Burrowes, D Jones, Rolfe-Johnson, Lloyd, D Thomas, English Baroque Soloists, Gardiner
Erato 2292-45982-2 (2 CDs) $$ DDD
Highlights: **Erato/Warner 4509985152 $$ DDD**

Where'er you walk • Act 1 (t)
O sleep, why dost thou leave me • Act 2 (s)

Apart from 'Ombra mai fu' (Handel's 'Largo') in *Serse*, no CD version of which exists, the only arias from Handel's operas which are really well known both come from *Semele*. 'O sleep, why dost thou leave me' is one of the most difficult arias around and the early John McCormack recording of this soprano aria is justly famous for its extraordinary agility of voice in lengthy phrases, compared with which 'Il mio tesoro' is easy. No tenor would, of course, sing the title role in this opera; his part is Jupiter, not Semele. Strictly speaking, *Semele* is a secular oratorio, described by Handel as a 'dramatic entertainment'. It was composed after Handel, who was his own impresario, decided that he could no longer afford to provide scenery, costumes and ballets for his operas and began to stage them in concert form. *Semele* is his only stage work in English which can truly be described as an opera. The text comes from a Congreve satirical libretto described by its non-musical author as 'an opera'.

Strangely, in this age of original instruments and scores, the Gardiner recording on Erato is cut heavily, while the original score, using modern instruments, on DG is not. The latter also has a more famous cast and is very much better in every way. But the Erato is on two medium-priced CDs, while the DG has three at full price. And Gardiner's set is far from bad.

<u>The Plot</u> Semele is the lover of Jupiter, who prevents her marriage to Athamas. Juno (Mrs Jupiter) is annoyed, as any good spouse would be, and causes Semele to demand that Jupiter appear to her as a god and not as a man. She claims that this will make her, Semele, a

Handel

goddess. Semele falls into the trap; the story is false, and Juno crows as Jupiter has to eat humble pie.

HUMPERDINCK, Engelbert (1854–1921)

Hänsel und Gretel ★★★ R

Gruberová, Murray, G Jones, Grundheber, Dresden Staatskapelle, Davis
Philips 438 013-2 (2 CDs) $$$ DDD

Ziesak, Larmore, Behrens, Weikl, Bavarian Radio SO, Runnicles
Teldec 4509-94549-2 (2 CDs) $$$ DDD
Highlights: **EMI CDC7 54327-2 $$$ DDD**

Bonney, Von Otter, Lipovšek, Schwarz, Hendricks, Lind, A Schmidt, Bavarian Radio SO, Tate
EMI CDS7 54022-2 (2 CDs) $$$ DDD

Schwarzkopf, Grümmer, Ilosvay, Metternich, Philharmonia O, Karajan
EMI CMS7 69293-2 (mono) (2 CDs) $$ ADD

Abendsegen (Prayer) • *Act 1 (s, ms)*
Dance Duet • *Act 1 (s, ms)*
Overture & Dream Pantomime (orchestra)

That the most popular children's opera ever written should have Wagnerian overtones is hardly considered these days. Yet there is no question that the man who was Wagner's assistant during the composition of *Parsifal*, who is said to have written some linking passages of it, broke away from the traditions of German light opera. He may have used actual folk songs in the score, but the treatment of everything is Wagnerian—the famous overture and the Dream Pantomime prove this. The orchestration is ridiculously symphonic for a simple fairy tale, but Humperdinck made it all work. The best way to describe it is: Wagner with tunes. *Hänsel und Gretel* is difficult to stage in these modern times, but on disc the imagination takes over and this is one opera which is actually better in recorded form than on stage. And Humperdinck has been luckier than many a more famous composer in the recordings his masterpiece has received over the years.

For once, it is hard to make a choice from the half-dozen available CD sets. This is not an opera for great singers, but great artists, and many a vocally less technically outstanding singer can and does act magnificently. The 1953 mono set has been included, not because it stars Schwarzkopf as Gretel and Karajan in the pit, but because it is a wonderful performance and the absence of stereo sound will bother only hi-fi buffs. All recommendations are made without reservation, the first two having appeared within three months of each other less than a year ago. The Philips set is more lushly Wagnerian, while the Teldec is more delicate, but you can't go wrong with any of these!

The Plot Hänsel and Gretel are sent into the forest by their mother to gather strawberries. They lose their way and sleep under the trees. On waking hungry, they find a gingerbread house and and eat parts of it. Its owner, however, is an evil witch, who captures Hänsel and tries to fatten him for her oven. The children trick her and she ends up in the oven instead.

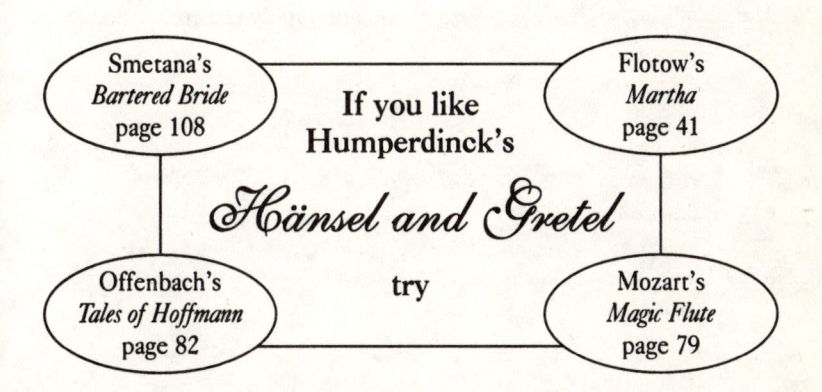

If you like Humperdinck's *Hänsel and Gretel* try

- Smetana's *Bartered Bride* page 108
- Flotow's *Martha* page 41
- Offenbach's *Tales of Hoffmann* page 82
- Mozart's *Magic Flute* page 79

KÁLMÁN, Emmerich (1882–1953)

Die Csárdásfürstin (The Gypsy Princess) ★★★ C I

Rothenberger, Gedda, Anheisser, Graunke SO, Mattes
EMI CDM7 69672-2 (2 CDs) $$ ADD
Highlights: **CDM7 69600-2 $$ ADD**

Gräfin Mariza (Countess Maritza) ★★★ C I

Rothenberger, Gedda, Moser, Graunke SO, Mattes
EMI CDM7 69675-2 (2 CDs) $$ ADD
Highlights: **EMI CDM7 69599-2 $$ ADD**

Highlights (in English): Hill Smith, R Remedios, Barber, Sadler's Wells O, Wordsworth
TER CDTE 1007 $$$ DDD

The operettas of Emmerich, or Imre, Kálmán may have been written in German, but he was more Hungarian than his countryman Franz Lehár. Apart from *The Merry Widow*°, the above two works are probably performed more often than any of the many written by Lehár. The two German sets are unlikely ever to be bettered and the English one is close behind. Both contain umpteen familiar tunes, though few can be named by the average person apart from *Mariza*'s 'Play, Gypsy'. Most enjoyable and highly recommended.

KERN, Jerome (1885–1945)

Show Boat ★★★ C I

Stratas, Von Stade, Hadley, Hubbard, London Sinfonia, McGlinn
EMI CDS7 49108-2 (3 CDs) $$$ DDD
Highlights: **CDC7 49847-2 $$$ DDD**

J Kelly, Burgess, Howard, White, National SO, Edwards
TER CDTER 21199 (2 CDs) $$$ DDD

Highlights: Clayton, Fredericks, Spencer, O, McArthur
Sony SK 53330 $$$ ADD

Ol' man river • Act 1 (ba)
Make believe • Act 1 (t, s)
Can't help lovin' dat man • Act 1 (s)
Why do I love you? • Act 2 (s, t)

Here is a perfect example of the breakdown of the barriers between opera and operetta or the musical. A full-price three-CD set of a 1927 musical produced with all the detail and care of any Mozart or Wagner opera, which has been a best-seller since it first appeared in 1988! The leading singers may be as happy in the opera house as in this musical, but this is without question a properly composed piece of musical theatre belonging to the *opéra-comique* genre—often with accompanied spoken dialogue. Its 'arias' have been around for 68 years and are as fresh as ever. In what way does this differ from an opera?

The performance and recording of the more than complete EMI set are both superlative and the elaborate booklet is more comprehensive than most opera libretti. There are three hours and forty-two minutes of music, including all the songs which were written for *Show Boat* before and after its original opening in 1927. The music lends itself easily to the operatic voices of Von Stade and Hadley. And Teresa Stratas as Julie is a luxury bonus indeed. Bruce Hubbard may not be a familiar name, but Paul Robeson would have approved of his 'Ol' Man River'.

On only two CDs instead of three, the alternative is much cheaper and nearly as good vocally, but lacks the additional numbers and dialogue. This is the 1946 new version, beautifully sung, but very much shorter.

Kern

> **The Plot** The gambler Gaylord Ravenal falls for Magnolia, the daughter of the captain of a show boat on the Mississippi River. Julie, the wife of the leading man, has been reported as being of mixed blood and their marriage is considered a crime. They leave and Ravenal takes the husband's place in the show. Over the years the gambler loses all his money and deserts Magnolia and their child. She makes a career in show business elsewhere, but ultimately returns to the show boat, where the repentant Ravenal is reunited with her and their now fully grown daughter.

KORNGOLD, Erich Wolfgang (1897–1957)

Die tote Stadt (The Dead City) ★ C d

Neblett, Kollo, Luxon, Prey, Munich Radio O, Leinsdorf
BMG/RCA GD 877767 (2 CDs) $$ ADD

Glück, das mir verblieb • Act 1 (t, s)
Mein Sehnen, mein Wähnen • Act 2 (b)
Ich werde sie nicht wiedersehen • Act 3 (t)

This is the most talked about and least often performed opera of all. The great duet which heads the above list has been a best-seller since Richard Tauber and Lotte Lehmann recorded it in the twenties and everybody wants to see this glorious music on stage. Unfortunately, it belongs to the arty mysticism of post-World War I. Korngold was only twenty-three when he chose this strange dreamlike tale, which is really more suited to film than the stage, and no revival of *Die tote Stadt* has yet set the world on fire. There are some glorious moments in it and the only complete recording is a fine one; Carol Neblett and René Kollo make a good fist of the leading couple and Hermann Prey has always used the baritone aria as a showpiece for his voice. The music comes off best on CD perhaps, with a libretto in the hand, rather than in the theatre. Korngold produces some truly eerie effects, which are better imagined than seen.

> **The Plot** Paul mourns the loss of his wife Marie in a special room devoted to her memory. He meets Marietta, a dancer, who is the living image of the dead woman. They live in Bruges, a ghostly decaying city of canals, on which strange mummers divert themselves.

Marietta seduces Paul, but mocks his dead wife by braiding her revered strands of hair around her neck. Paul strangles her. The next morning Marietta arrives on the doorstep to collect the umbrella she left behind. Was it all a dream?

LEHÁR, Franz (1870–1948)

Der Graf von Luxemburg (The Count of Luxemburg) ★★ R I

Popp, Holm, Gedda, Böhme, Graunke SO, Mattes
EMI CMS5 65375-2 (2 CDs) $$ ADD

Highlights (in English): Hill-Smith, Jenkins, Tierney, Richard, Sadler's Wells O, Wordsworth
TER CDTER 1050 $$$ DDD

Bist du's, lachendes Glück • Act 2 (t, s)
Ein Trèfle incarnat • Act 2 (t)
Heut' noch werd' ich Ehefrau • Act 1 (s)
Mädel klein, Mädel fein (Waltz) • Act 2 (t, s)

Sadly, Lehár's once second most popular operetta, *The Count of Luxemburg*, is rarely heard these days. Yet the complete recording is excellent in every way and the highlights in English are fine.

The Plot Prince Basil wants to marry Angèle. They arrange a mock-marriage to an aristocrat so that she may acquire a title; a prince can wed an ex-countess, but not a commoner. The money-short Count of Luxemburg marries Angèle, agreeing to be divorced after three months. He is not even allowed to see his bride; they are divided at the ceremony, exchanging rings through a paper curtain. Later the Count meets Angèle and falls in love with his own wife.

Lehár

Das Land des Lächelns (The Land of Smiles) ★★★ R I

Schwarzkopf, Loose, Gedda, Kunz, Philharmonia O, Ackermann
EMI CHS7 69523-2 (mono) (2 CDs) $$ ADD

Rothenberger, Holm, Gedda, Graunke SO, Mattes
EMI CMS5 65372-2 (2 CDs) $$ ADD

Highlights: Donath, Lindner, Jerusalem, Munich Radio O, Boskovsky
EMI CDM7 69597-2 $$ DDD

Dein ist mein ganzes Herz (You are my heart's delight) • *Act 2 (t)*
Immer nur lächeln (Patiently smiling) • *Act 1 (t)*
Wer hat die Liebe uns ins Herz gesenkt • *Act 2 (t & s)*
Mit Apfelblüten einen Kranz • *Act 2 (t)*

This is Lehár's most operatic score, with a stream of glorious tenor solos and duets. The oriental setting and outdated racial (im)moralities of the plot make it hard to revive, but they are no bar to enjoying the music alone. *The Land of Smiles* was written specifically for Richard Tauber, who was partly crippled by polio; Prince Sou-Chong's hands were always hidden in the wide sleeves of his costume and he rarely had to move. 'You are my heart's delight' was the most famous of the Lehár Tauber songs. Unfortunately, a complete recording with Tauber was never made.

Once again, the early EMI mono recording with Schwarzkopf is the best, though Gedda also, and rightly, became the regular partner for Anneliese Rothenberger in a whole series of superb LP recordings. Their set is very good indeed. The DDD highlights feature Siegfried Jerusalem, a real Siegfried at Bayreuth today.

The Plot The charming Chinese diplomat Prince Sou-Chong and the Austrian Countess Lisa fall in love and marry. When he returns to China she discovers that he already has four other wives. His protestations of love for her alone are not enough. Although he has the power to keep her in China, his love for her is great enough to accept that their cultures can never meet. He allows her to return to Vienna.

Lehár

Die lustige Witwe (The Merry Widow) ★★★ C1

Schwarzkopf, Steffek, Waechter, Gedda, Philharmonia O, Matačić
EMI CDS7 47178-2 (2 CDs) $$$ ADD

Schwarzkopf, Loose, Kunz, Gedda, Philharmonia O, Ackermann
EMI CDH7 69520-2 (mono) $$ ADD

Studer, Bonney, Skovhus, Trost, VPO, Gardiner
DG 439 911-2 $$$ DDD

Highlights: Harwood, Stratas, Kollo, Hollweg, BPO, Karajan
DG 415 524-2 $$$ ADD

Vilja • Act 2 (s)
Lippen schweigen (Waltz) • Act 3 (t or b, s)
Dann geh' ich in's Maxim • Act 1 (t or b)
Wie eine Rosenknospe • Act 2 (s, t)

Lehár's masterpiece is as lively as ever ninety years after its creation. The reason clearly lies in the music, which by now has jumped the fence into the field of opera, just as Johann Strauss' *Die Fledermaus*° did many years ago. As with any comic opera, understanding the words is really essential, for there are two sets of lovers and, arguably, the young ones have as unhappy an end as many in grand opera, though they do not die; Valencienne remains married to someone else.

My selections include two classic sets in German, both starring Elisabeth Schwarzkopf, the later one more complete than the earlier, which occupies only one CD. There is only one modern DDD version worth having. Made in 1994, it is conducted by an expert in baroque music (!), John Elliot Gardiner, and is complete on one excellent CD, including dialogue, in very fancy packing. It was performed beautifully in Vienna by a largely unfamiliar cast of new singers, led by Cheryl Studer as the Widow and Barbara Bonney as Valencienne. Two older ones feature Australians in the title role. June Bronhill (Classics for Pleasure CfP 4485 $ ADD) is great, while Sutherland (Decca 421 884-2 $$ ADD) is not at her very best.

The Plot The widowed Hanna Glawari is supposed to save her country, a small Balkan republic, by refusing her many suitors in Paris in favour of a Pontevedrian. She had married a rich man instead of her lover, Danilo, who had drowned his disappointment in wine, women

Lehár

and song. Now his government asks him to marry Hanna and he does still love her. Hanna helps two youngsters in love by taking the girl's place when there is a danger of her elderly husband finding out about the affair. There are the usual misunderstandings, but the budget of Pontevedria is saved by Danilo and Hanna. Would that Canberra could find a Merry Widow!

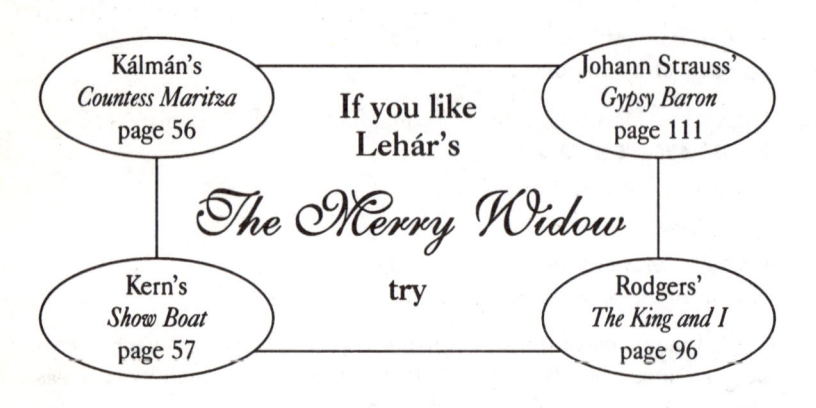

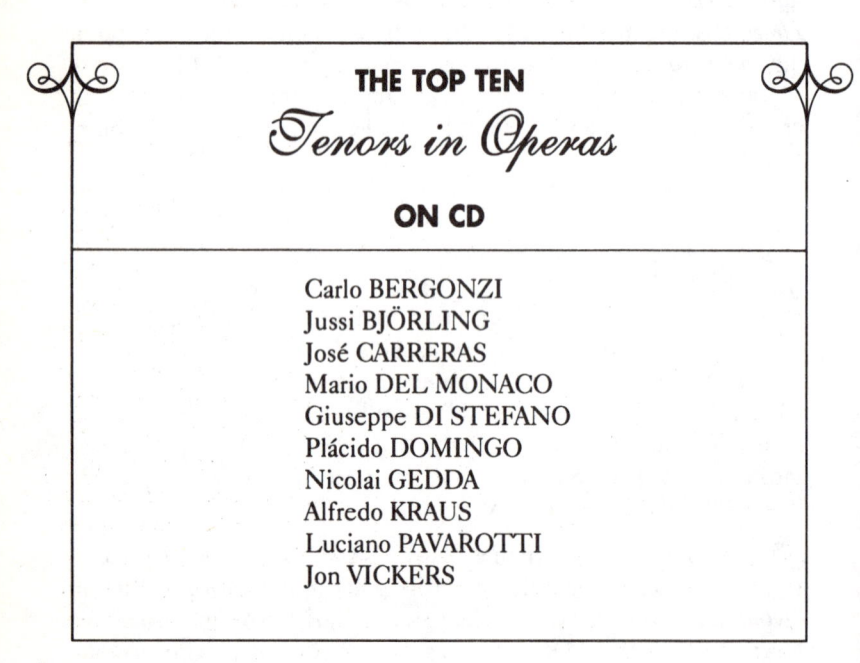

If you like Lehár's *The Merry Widow* try:

- Kálmán's *Countess Maritza* page 56
- Johann Strauss' *Gypsy Baron* page 111
- Kern's *Show Boat* page 57
- Rodgers' *The King and I* page 96

THE TOP TEN
Tenors in Operas
ON CD

Carlo BERGONZI
Jussi BJÖRLING
José CARRERAS
Mario DEL MONACO
Giuseppe DI STEFANO
Plácido DOMINGO
Nicolai GEDDA
Alfredo KRAUS
Luciano PAVAROTTI
Jon VICKERS

LEONCAVALLO, Ruggero (1857–1919)

Pagliacci ★★★ R d

Martinucci, Gauci, Tumagian, Bratislava Radio SO, Rahbari
Naxos 8.660021 $ DDD

Bergonzi, Carlyle, Taddei, La Scala Milan, Karajan (with Mascagni *Cavalleria rusticana*° and 10 intermezzos)
DG 419 257-2 (3 CDs) $$$ ADD

Pavarotti, Freni, Wixell, National PO, Patané (with Mascagni *Cavalleria rusticana*)
Decca 414 897-2 (2 CDs) $$$ ADD
Highlights from both operas: **Decca 421 870-2 $$ ADD**

Domingo, Caballé, Milnes, LSO, Santi (with Puccini *Il tabarro*°)
BMG/RCA GD 60865 (2 CDs) $$ ADD

Vesti la giubba (On with the motley) • Act 1 (t)
Prologue (b)
No, pagliaccio non son • Act 2 (t)
Stridono lassu • Act 1 (s)
Nedda! Silvio! • Act 1 (b & s)

One of the most famous, most unified and shortest operas to capture the hearts of the world's public. Leoncavallo wrote his own libretto, resulting in an ideal blend of words and music. He may not have been a Mozart or Puccini, but *Pagliacci*, with Mascagni's *Cavalleria rusticana* (the 'Immortal Twins') started the vogue for verismo operas, supposedly leading the art form into the field of reflecting real life. It has hardly led to anything lasting, unless you count Puccini as a verismo composer, which can be legitimately claimed. None of Leoncavallo's other operas survives, except in occasional festival performances. Like Mascagni, he was a one-shot composer as far as history is concerned. Many of his other operas contain memorable moments, but none has the appeal of *Pagliacci*, the plot of which is based on a real-life event which occurred during Leoncavallo's childhood. He moulded this into a unified continuum which does not have a dull moment and on CD there is no place for the stupid applause which in the theatre usually interrupts the magnificent orchestral play-out after 'Vesti la giubba'. In this case a synopsis is all that is needed; the music speaks for itself.

Leoncavallo

Luciano Pavarotti's popularity has caused him to record the opera again for Philips on a new single-disc version, which is really not up to scratch (434 131-2 $$$ DDD). A super-bargain-priced Naxos CD is very good, except for minor failings by, unfortunately, the tenor—Martinucci has a fine voice, but his singing is provincial. Yet at this minimal price it is a better bet than the full-priced single-CD Pavarotti. The unusual coupling of Domingo's set with Puccini's *Tabarro* works well, though the Puccini opera has no famous arias, unless you count the forty-five seconds which are used as the theme of Radio National's *Singers of Renown*. Musically, by far the best is the Karajan double-bill of 1966, which may be on three full-price CDs, but is superbly sung, recorded and, most importantly, conducted. I doubt whether this set will ever be bettered. Karajan takes the music so slowly that it will not fit on two CDs and the rest of the third disc contains ten lovely opera intermezzi.

[The Plot] Canio, the head of a group of travelling actors, is an insanely jealous husband, and with good cause. His wife Nedda is carrying on with one Silvio, while the cripple Tonio also makes advances, which she rejects. During a performance on a portable stage, before an audience of villagers, Canio kills Nedda and then Silvio, when he runs to help her.

LLOYD WEBBER, Andrew (1948–)

The Phantom of the Opera ★★★ M d

Brightman, Crawford, Barton, original cast, Read
Polydor 831 273-2 (2 CDs) $$$ DDD
Highlights: **Polydor 831 563-2 $$$ DDD**

The Music of the Night • Act 1 (t)
All I ask of you • Act 1 (b)
The Phantom of the Opera • Act 1 (t)
Think of me • Act 1 (s)

Here is truly an opera without any spoken dialogue. Academics may say that the music is inferior or derivative, but you cannot deny its operatic nature—and the fact that it is set in the Paris Opéra building has nothing to do with it. Voices of operatic quality must be available for the opera-within-the-opera—the whole thing revolves around a young soprano's appearances on the stage of the Opéra—and all the music is written to be sung as straight as that of any traditional work of the genre. The story, blessedly true to the original classic by Gaston Leroux (unlike the many films which are called by the same name), carries the familiar story of the misshapen lover who cannot reach fulfilment to a logical conclusion. The musical ensembles, which are not among the hits, are superb; the scene in the office of the Opéra's managers is as complex as anything you will find in a Verdi opera and it works extremely well. And that is the secret of these operatic musicals: they are enjoyable for more than just the big numbers for which everybody waits. Many other Lloyd Webber musicals are revived regularly, but their life on CD is ephemeral; at one stage there were thirteen different *Evita* CDs on sale (including those in foreign languages), but none of the English ones survive in the catalogues. The more obviously operatic *Phantom* may have a better future on disc.

The title role was created by the unlikely, but incredibly versatile, Michael Crawford and he does sing it very well. It is a moot point whether major opera singers like Peter Hofmann in Germany or Anthony Warlow in Australia would not, or did not, sing it better, but it is unlikely that another complete recording of *The Phantom of the Opera* will ever appear.

The Plot Deep in the bowels of the Paris Opéra lives the grotesquely disfigured Phantom, who falls in love with the young soprano Christine. His efforts to help her career by terrorising the management and staff of the opera house are successful, but his pathetic attempt to gain the love of the woman for whom he has composed an opera of his own is doomed. He obtains her pity, allows her to return to her lover, but has disappeared by the time his pursuers have discovered his lair.

LOESSER, Frank (1910–1969)

Guys and Dolls ★★★ M I

De Gutzman, Prince, Gallagher, Lane, 1992 Broadway cast, E Strauss
BMG/RCA 09026 61317-2 $$$ DDD

Luck be a lady • *Act 2 (t or b)*
Sit down, you're rocking the boat • *Act 2 (t or b)*
I've never been in love before • *Act 1 (t or b, s)*
If I were a bell • *Act 2 (s)*

A little American for some tastes, *Guys and Dolls* is in many ways an ideal musical. Loesser followed it with *The Most Happy Fella*, which failed because it was too operatic at a time when people did not yet understand the link between the two media. *Guys and Dolls* found a market because of its fine Damon Runyon story, hit numbers and sheer entertainment value. The film starring Frank Sinatra further established it as a perennial favourite. There is only one CD of it at present, but it is a good one in a whole series of recent reconstructions of the great musicals of years gone by.

The Plot Sky Masterson will bet on anything. When he is challenged to take a Salvation Army lass, Miss Sarah Brown, to Havana within twenty-four hours, he wagers that he can—and does so by promising to deliver a dozen genuine sinners to the mission, which is threatened with closure. She accepts and he makes good his promise by entering a crap game in which he bets the gamblers' souls against his money; each loser has to go to the mission and join the Salvos. One by one the mission hall fills and, being at ease among their own kind, the gamblers put the mission on its feet. Sky and Sarah, naturally, get married.

LOEWE, Frederick (1901–1988)

Brigadoon ★★★ M d

Luker, Barrett, Ainsley, Kaye, London Sinfonia, McGlinn
EMI CDC7 54481-2 $$$ DDD

Bell, Brooks, Sullivan, Britton, original Broadway cast, Allers
RCA GD 81001 (mono) $$ ADD

Charisse, G Kelly, V Johnson, film soundtrack
EMI CDMGM2 $$$ ADD

Almost like being in love • Act 1 (b)
Heather on the hill • Act 1 (b, s)
Come to me, bend to me • Act 1 (t)
Waitin' for my dearie • Act 1 (s)

This is decidedly a serious musical, even though it belongs to the light musical theatre. There is an excellent comedienne who has no bearing on the story and was clearly inserted solely for light relief. The music of *Brigadoon* may not be profound, but it has the right supernatural feeling for its romantic ghost story and the melodies never stop.

On stage the male leading part was usually entrusted to a fine baritone, though the first Tommy, David Brooks, was no more than adequate. A lot can be said for original casts; however, not only is this one a very old mono recording, but the modern set has better singers. Furthermore, the lengthy ballet scenes are missing on the RCA. As for the film soundtrack: for a baritone, Gene Kelly was a very good dancer on CD.

The Plot Tommy, an American, accidentally finds himself in the legendary Scottish village of Brigadoon, which disappeared in 1747. The lives of its inhabitants continue at the rate of one day every hundred years and Tommy has stumbled on it during the current resurrection. He falls for a local lass, Fiona, and ultimately returns to Brigadoon to become part of the legend.

Loewe

My Fair Lady ★★★ M I

Andrews, Harrison, Weir, Holloway, original cast, Ornadel
Columbia CK 05090 $$$ ADD

Te Kanawa, Irons, Hadley, W Mitchell, LSO, Mauceri
Decca 421 200-2 $$$ DDD

Nixon (for Audrey Hepburn), Harrison, B Shirley (for Jeremy Brett), Holloway, film soundtrack, Previn
Sony SK 66711 $$ ADD

I could have danced all night • Act 1 (s)
On the street where you live • Act 1 (t)
Wouldn't it be loverly • Act 1 (s)
With a little bit of luck • Act 1 (b)

The famous musical which demonstrates more clearly than any other how the light musical theatre has invaded the opera house. *My Fair Lady*, along with *Kiss Me, Kate°*, *Fiddler on the Roof* and the rest have been in the repertoire of German opera houses for decades, even though they demand few operatic voices. Australian companies also have staged musicals like *West Side Story°* and *The King and I°*. Frederick Loewe and earlier American light music composers such as Sigmund Romberg and Victor Herbert were born in, or learned their craft in, Europe. The music of each reflects a sound academic background.

My Fair Lady does not demand a singing Professor Higgins, because the part was tailor-made for Rex Harrison, who had no vocal aspirations. On the other hand, Eliza Doolittle, designed for the fine soprano of Julie Andrews, gives ample scope for a Kiri Te Kanawa and the suitor Freddy has an aria which demands a full tenor voice. *My Fair Lady* may not be the vehicle for vocal splendour, but it is one of the brightest and most enjoyable of our modern 'operas'. The original cast and soundtrack recordings easily beat the only DDD recording in spite of two major opera stars and Warren Mitchell as Professor Higgins.

The Plot Professor Higgins, an expert in languages, makes a bet that he can transform the cockney flower-girl Eliza, daughter of a dustman, into a lady. He succeeds of course, in the famous 'The rain in Spain' sequence, but the strange attraction between the opposites of the dry academic and the cocky cockney remains unresolved, even though Eliza does return to Higgins at the end.

MASCAGNI, Pietro (1963–1945)

Cavalleria rusticana ★★★ R d

Scotto, Domingo, Elvira, National PO, Levine
BMG/RCA RD 83091 $$$ ADD

Callas, Di Stefano, Panerai, La Scala Milan, Serafin
CDS7 47981-2 (mono) $$$ ADD

Tebaldi, Björling, Bastianini, Maggio Musicale Fiorentino, Erede
Decca 425 985-2 $$ ADD

See also Leoncavallo *Pagliacci*

Addio alla madre (t)
Voi lo sapete, mamma (s)
Easter Hymn (s, ch)
Viva il vino (Brindisi) (t, ch)
Siciliana (t)

The work which initiated the verismo movement remains Mascagni's only universally popular opera, though several of his other fifteen have been recorded over the years. Like its usual partner on operatic bills, *Pagliacci*, it is continuously melodic, from the beautiful orchestral protrayal of dawn at the beginning to the violently dramatic ending. The Intermezzo is probably more famous than any of the arias and the 'Easter Hymn' is really a choral piece with only a brief appearance by the soprano. The 'Immortal Twins', as *Cavalleria* and *Pagliacci* are known, are the most fool-proof introduction to opera which the novice can find. As both works are short, there is none of the padding which besets some of the world's greatest full-length masterpieces. *Cavalleria* is a full-blooded opera which needs full-blooded singing. Its easy, flowing story is so simple that it can be told in one sentence.

Mascagni

Few of the best CDs available today (no less than fourteen at the moment!) can compete seriously with the above, but it is worth considering the full-priced three-CD set by Karajan on DG (419 257-2), which stars Carlo Bergonzi in both operas, and offers a beautiful batch of ten intermezzos to fill the third disc. Karajan brings magic to the music of both operas and gets fine performances from all his singers.

| The Plot | Turiddu has seduced poor, loudly complaining Santuzza and discarded her in favour of Lola, the wife of Alfio, who kills him in a duel.

MASSENET, Jules (1842–1912)

Manon ★★ R d

Cotrubas, Kraus, Quilico, Toulouse Capitole O, Plasson
EMI CDS7 49610-2 (3 CDs) $$$ DDD

De los Angeles, Legay, Dens, Paris Opéra-Comique, Monteux (with Chausson: *Poème de l'amour et de la mer*)
EMI CMS7 63549 (mono) (3 CDs) $$ ADD

En fermant les yeux (The Dream) • Act 2 (t)
Ah! fuyez, douce image • Act 3 (t)
Adieu, notre petite table • Act 2 (s)
Profitons bien de la jeunesse (Gavotte) • Act 3 (s)

A hundred years on, people are still mixing up Massenet's *Manon* with Puccini's *Manon Lescaut*° and sopranos are still recording the 'Laughing Song' from Auber's *Manon Lescaut*. Massenet's version of the old story is certainly the most 'French' interpretation of this classic love story or, rather, tale of sexual passions. Manon thinks money is the only road to happiness, and sells her body to get it, while still retaining her love for the first man who seduced her, the Chevalier des Grieux. Inevitably, all operas on the subject deal with romantic rather than sexual love and Manon duly dies, like most operatic heroines. Massenet's lovers are less passionate than Puccini's, whose version is decidedly melodramatic. He also makes less severe vocal demands on his singers. Yet *Manon* is probably the more difficult opera to bring off. It demands a degree of musical and dramatic subtlety to bring home the bacon. The music drifts along romantically—and beautiful tones are more important than top Cs.

Massenet's most popular opera has only been recorded six times since records were invented and three of those are still obtainable. A French one of 1928 on two CDs (Féraldy/Rogatchewsky, Conifer 150 012) would interest only history buffs. The best performance is the 1955 mono recording starring Victoria de los Angeles and the most sensitive conductor, Pierre Monteux. The only modern recording is very good too and, of course, has much better sound.

| The Plot | The Chevalier des Grieux falls in love with innocent Manon and they set up house together. Manon is tempted by the good life and, when des Grieux is abducted by his father, she has no problems finding richer lovers. The two meet again in a gaming hall in which both are arrested. Manon is to be deported and becomes seriously ill. Des Grieux tries to have her released, but she dies in his arms.

Werther ★★ R d

Von Stade, Buchanan, Carreras, Allen, CGO, Davis
Philips 416 654-2 (2 CDs) $$$ ADD

De los Angeles, Mesplé, Gedda, Soyer, O de Paris, Prêtre
EMI CMS7 63973-2 (2 CDs) $$ ADD

Troyanos, Barbaux, Kraus, Manuguerra, LPO, Plasson
EMI CMS7 69573-2 (2 CDs) $$ ADD
Highlights: **EMI CDM7 63936-2 $$ ADD**

Pourquoi me réveiller • *Act 3 (t)*
Letter Aria • *Act 3 (ms)*
O nature (Invocation) • *Act 1 (t)*
J'aurais sur ma poitrine (Désolation) • *Act 2 (t)*

A French opera which was first performed in German, in Vienna, because Paris could not see the point of this tragedy by Goethe, a very German poet. Surprisingly, it is now Massenet's only opera, apart from *Manon°*, which is performed regularly. With a mezzo-soprano lead, the tenor title role has all the best arias; more than the three listed above! Werther's morbid subject is hardly exhilarating fare, but the music keeps it alive. Or is it the fact that it is comparatively cheap to stage?

Massenet

On CD it is the music alone which matters, yet it is hardly a best-seller. Domingo and Carreras have CD sets to their credit, but Domingo's is already deleted, instead of being reduced to mid-price. Carreras (before his illness) had the fine Frederica von Stade as his Charlotte and Isobel Buchanan, shortly after her Australian career, as Sophie. The older Victoria de los Angeles set is vocally fine, but the conductor is not as good as Colin Davis. Still, it is cheaper.

| The Plot | Werther falls in love with Charlotte, who, at her dying mother's request, marries his friend Albert instead. Their common love for poetry brings them together again after her marriage and Werther's passion is rekindled. But Werther and Albert are honest men, who know how to do the right thing. Werther borrows Albert's pistols to commit suicide and dies happily as Charlotte declares that she has always returned his love.

MILLÖCKER, Karl (1842–1899)

Der Bettelstudent (The Beggar Student) ★★★ R I

Streich, Holm, Gedda, Prey, Graunke SO, Allers
EMI CMS5 65387-2 (2 CDs) $$ ADD

Ach, ich hab' sie ja nur auf die Schulter geküsst • Act 1 (ba)
Ich hab' kein Geld • Act 3 (t)
Ich knüpfte manche zarte Bande • Act 1 (t)
Ich setz' den Fall • Act 2 (t, s)

This is the operetta which should have been written by Johann Strauss, who was talked out of it in favour of *A Night in Venice*. It made the fortune of Karl Millöcker instead. He was no Waltz King, but produced a series of fine stage works. This magnificently cast recording clearly shows how an unknown came to be famous overnight.

| The Plot | Laura has slapped Colonel Ollendorff's face. In revenge, he disguises Symon, a young prisoner, as the rich 'Count Wybicki', who successfully woos Laura, only to be 'exposed' by Ollendorff. But revolutionaries are plotting his downfall; they extract 200 000 florins from him in exchange for Duke Adam, the real ruler of Poland, and then pretend that Symon is the duke. When the real one suddenly arrives, Symon gets the money and Laura as well.

Gasparone ★★★ R1

Rothenberger, Fuchs, Prey, Finke, Wewel, Munich Radio O, Wallberg
EMI CMS5 65363-2 (2 CDs) $$ DDD

Dunkelrote Rosen • Act 2 (b)
Der verdammte Gasparone • Act 1 (ba)
O dass ich doch ein Räuber wär • Act 1 (b)

Millöcker has two complete operettas on CD, compared with Johann Strauss' one! No Waltz King, Millöcker was a direct competitor in the field of operetta. Gasparone is a close cousin to Auber's *Fra Diavolo*, a tale of an imaginary bandit who turns out to be the governor of Sicily. So what else is new? Very tuneful!

THE TOP TEN
Baritones in Operas
ON CD

Renato BRUSON
Piero CAPPUCCILLI
Vladimir CHERNOV
Tito GOBBI
Dimitri HVOROSTOVSKY
Robert MERRILL
Sherrill MILNES
James MORRIS
Bryn TERFEL
José VAN DAM

Mozart

MOZART, Wolfgang Amadeus (1756–1791)

Così fan tutte ★★ A c

Mattila, Von Otter, Araiza, Allen, ASMF, Marriner
Philips 422 381-2 (3 CDs) $$$ DDD

Schwarzkopf, Merriman, Simoneau, Panerai, Philharmonia O, Karajan
EMI CHS7 69635-2 (mono) (3 CDs) $$ ADD
Highlights: **EMI CDM7 64800-2 $$ ADD**

Caballé, Baker, Gedda, Ganzarolli, CGO, Davis
Philips 422 542-2 (3 CDs) $$ ADD

Highlights: Te Kanawa, Murray, Blochwitz, Hampson, VPO, Levine
DG 431 290-2 $$ DDD

Come scoglio • *Act 1 (s)*
Soave il vento • *Act 1 (s, ms, b)*
Un' aura amorosa • *Act 1 (t)*
Donne mie, la fate a tanti • *Act 2 (b)*

Once denigrated as being immoral, and rarely performed, *Così fan tutte* today is almost as popular as *The Marriage of Figaro*° or *Don Giovanni*°; and that is not surprising. The music is as tuneful as anything Mozart ever wrote, but *Così*'s arias were rarely recorded until recent times and consequently its music is not as familiar as that of Mozart's more famous works. More famous? There are twenty-two different CD sets of *Così fan tutte* on the market, only two less than *The Marriage of Figaro*, even though some arias from the latter are known to everybody, while the average person cannot name even one from *Così*. In this case the sum is better than the parts. It is almost hopeless to choose the three 'best' recordings of *Così*; recording companies have been extremely fortunate in performances by their artists. Or could it be that, vocally at least, *Così* is easier to manage than *Figaro*?

My selection must necessarily be arbitrary in this case. Perhaps one or two of the singers or the conductor are known to the reader. In that case, the choice is yours. There is another recording headed by Schwarzkopf, but conducted by Böhm (EMI CMS7 69330-2, 3 CDs, $$ ADD), which is stereophonic and preferred by many to the earlier mono EMI I have chosen; and a fine 1994 Mackerras set (Telarc CD 80360 $$$ DDD) features the controversial random appogiaturas, which the average person would not even notice, but which Mozart wanted singers to add at will.

⸻ The Plot ⸻ Fiordiligi's and Dorabella's boyfriends make a bet with Don Alfonso that their girls are not like other women; they are true to them. The test involves the men dressing up as bearded Albanians and each tries to woo the fiancée of the other. Both succeed, but they reveal their true identities just before a double wedding ceremony. Nobody knows definitely how the dilemma is resolved. Possibly intentionally, Mozart pronounced a happy end without words which clearly state which girl gets which man. Only by implication can you deduce a return to the status quo; the girls promise to 'compensate their lovers' hearts'. Which lovers?

Don Giovanni ★★★ A d

Halgrimson, Dawson, A Schmidt, Yurisich, London Classical Players, Norrington
EMI CDS7 54255-2 (3 CDs) $$$ DDD

Organosova, Margiono, Gilfry, d'Arcangelo, English Baroque Soloists, Gardiner
Archiv 445 870-2 (3 CDs) $$$ DDD

Tomova-Sintow, Baltsa, Ramey, Furlanetto, Winbergh, BPO, Karajan
DG 419 179-2 93 (3 CDs) $$$ DDD
Highlights: **DG 419 635-2 $$$ DDD**

Sutherland, Schwarzkopf, Waechter, Taddei, Alva, Philharmonia O, Giulini
EMI CDS7 47260-2 (3 CDs) $$$ ADD
Highlights: **EMI CDM7 63078-2 $$ ADD**

Là ci darem la mano • *Act 1 (b, s)*
Il mio tesoro • *Act 2 (t)*
Dalla sua pace • *Act 1 (t)*
Madamina (Catalogue Aria) • *Act 1 (ba)*
Or sai chi l'onore • *Act 1 (s)*
Batti, batti • *Act 1 (s)*
Deh, vieni alla finestra • *Act 2 (b)*

Mozart

Mozart called *Don Giovanni* not an opera, but a *dramma giacoso*, a funny drama. There is certainly a lot of fun to be had in *Don Giovanni*, depending on the mood of the director and the tempi of the conductor. It is, in fact, a tragi-comedy. Don Giovanni is Italian for Don Juan, but in this very long opera he is not exactly very good at seducing women. He is involved with Zerlina, Donna Anna and Donna Elvira and fails to score with any of them. That failure can be interpreted in many ways. Giovanni can be an autocrat, a brute or the prey of conniving women. James Morris was hilarious when he played the part here in 1977. On disc, a lifted eyebrow does not mean very much. On the other hand, we get the best voices in the world in combinations we can never get here on stage.

In this case we are faced with no less than twenty-eight complete recordings and, when it comes to Mozart operas, the more recent sets are often very competitive; you don't have to have big voices to sing Mozart into a microphone. Sutherland and Schwarzkopf are better known than Halgrimson and Dawson, but are they better singers? No, not in terms of what is considered 'current practice'. There are so many alternatives that personal tastes and recommendations after discussion with a good retailer will determine your choice. The first two are modern 'original instruments', the others bigger scaled traditional performances.

The Plot Don Giovanni has had his way with Donna Anna and Donna Elvira before the curtain goes up. At the moment he is after the peasant girl Zerlina. He is hindered by the two viragos who are after his blood, Anna seeking revenge because Giovanni killed her father and Elvira because she wants him back. Zerlina has no such desire. The statue of the Commendatore, Anna's dad, stands above his grave and asks Giovanni to invite him to dinner. He does so. The statue actually arrives and promptly takes him down to hell.

Mozart

Die Entführung aus dem Serail
(The Abduction from the Seraglio) ★★ A|

Organosova, Sieden, Olsen, Hauptmann, English Baroque Soloists, Gardiner
DG 435 857-2 (2 CDs) $$$ ADD

Augér, Grist, Schreier, Neukirch, Moll, Dresden State O, Böhm
DG 429 868-2 (2 CDs) $$ ADD

Kenny, Watson, Schreier, Gähmlich, Salminen, Mozart O, Harnoncourt
Teldec 2292-42643-2 (2 CDs) $$$ DDD
Highlights: **Teldec 2292-42407-2 $$$ DDD**

Martern aller Arten • Act 2 (s)
O wie ängstlich • Act 1 (t)
Wer ein Liebchen hat gefunden • Act 1 (ba)
Vivat Bacchus • Act 2 (t, ba)

Mozart's first major success and a German, not Italian, opera. He always wanted to bring back the German Singspiel, a simple story told in German through spoken dialogue as well as music. His last opera, *Die Zauberflöte°*, is another example of the genre, but his *Seraglio*, while musically more primitive, at least has a sensible story and some of his best arias.

There are many more like the above, but the opera needs to be well sung and crisply conducted to make its full effect. Böhm has the strongest cast and conducts with his usual mastery. To top that, his is the only medium-price version. Gardiner strikes the happy medium between modern and original instrument recordings and his cast is led by the admirable Luba Organosova. The Harnoncourt has some fine singing in it, but neither recording nor performance is 100 per cent; only for fans of Kenny, Schreier and Salminen, all in good form.

The Plot Konstanze is held in the harem of a benevolent Pasha, who wants her to join his establishment voluntarily. Her boyfriend, Belmonte, arrives to save her, but the Pasha is a free-thinker who decides that it is wrong to hold people against their will and allows the lovers to go free.

Mozart

Le nozze di Figaro (The Marriage of Figaro) ★★★ A c

Te Kanawa, Popp, Von Stade, Ramey, Allen, LPO, Solti
Decca (3 CDs) 410 150-2 $$$ DDD
Highlights: **Decca 417 395-2 $$$ ADD**

Schwarzkopf, Moffo, Cossotto, Taddei, Waechter, Philharmonia O, Giulini
EMI CMS7 63266-2 (2 CDs) $$ ADD
Highlights: **CDM7 63409-2 $$ ADD**

Martinpelto, Hagley, Stephen, Terfel, Gilfry, English Baroque Soloists, Gardiner
Archiv 439 871-2 (3 CDs) $$$ DDD
Highlights: **Archiv 445 874-2 $$$ DDD**

Highlights: Norman, Freni, Minton, Ganzarolli, Wixell, BBC SO, Davis
Belart 450 047-2 $ ADD

Non più andrai • *Act 2 (b)*
Voi che sapete • *Act 3 (ms or s)*
Porgi amor • *Act 3 (s)*
Dove sono • *Act 3 (s)*
Se vuol ballare • *Act 1 (b)*

The first of the Mozart 'Big Three', written in collaboration with Lorenzo da Ponte. This is an operatic setting of the second of Baumarchais' three plays about Figaro. Paisiello had already written a setting of the first, *The Barber of Seville*, four years earlier; Rossini's version still lay in the distant future. The satirical aspects aimed at the excesses of the aristocracy appealed to Mozart and the result is probably the best of all his operas. The plot runs close to farce, but with music like Mozart's nobody minds the laughter which a good production can elicit. On disc, the visual aspects must be sought in the libretto. You are unlikely to guess that Cherubino is hiding in a chair while others chatter all around him, or, later, that the wrong person is behind a closed door. Such information must be acquired in advance. This applies to all comic operas, of course, but Mozart was one of the first to make the music fit the action and the musical reflection of the happenings are not as obvious as they became in operas written a hundred years later.

Out of two dozen *Figaros* I offer you three: an all-star performance of the kind most people want (Decca); a 'period' performance using a small orchestra of original instruments (Archiv) which is absolutely marvellous, but was recorded during a live performance, meaning audience noises; and a historic one with the inevitable Schwarzkopf (EMI). Take your pick. The Belart (ex-Philips) highlights are from another superb set and at super-bargain price!

The Plot Figaro is about to marry Susanna, but the Count Almaviva would like to exercise the no longer practised *droit de seigneur*, the right to sleep first with the brides of his servants. The Countess and Susanna plot to trick him into keeping an assignation with Susanna in the garden. The ladies then switch clothes. The miserable man finds that he is making love to his own wife, and his lecherous intentions are revealed publicly. Susanna and Figaro can marry without further worry.

Die Zauberflöte (The Magic Flute) ★★★ A d

Te Kanawa, Studer, Araiza, Bär, Ramey, ASMF, Marriner
Philips 426 276-2 (2 CDs) $$$ DDD
Highlights: **Philips 438 495-2 $$$ DDD**

Bonney, Jo, Streit, Cachemaille, Sigmundsson, Drottningholm O, Oestman
Oiseau-Lyre 440 085-2 (2 CDs) $$$ DDD

Norberg-Schulz, Kwon, Lippert, Tichy, Rydl, Budapest Failoni O, Halász
Naxos 8.660030/1 (2 CDs) $ DDD

Highlights: Mathis, Ott, Araiza, Hornik, Van Dam, BPO, Karajan
DG 431 291-2 $$ DDD

Dies Bildnis ist bezaubernd schön • Act 1 (t)
Der Hölle Rache • Act 2 (s)
Der Vogelfänger bin ich ja • Act 1 (b)
O Isis und Osiris • Act 2 (ba)
Bei Männern welche Liebe fühlen • Act 1 (b, s)

Forget about any deep philosophical significance of *The Magic Flute*. A well-known actor/manager, Emanuel Schikaneder,

Mozart

wrote a play in 1791 and commissioned Mozart to write music for it. That is the only ascertainable fact about *The Magic Flute*—the rest is speculation. There is neither rhyme nor reason to the story, which reverses the characters of the Queen and the Night and Sarastro at the halfway point. The opera was staged in a primitive barn theatre and was intended to be little more than a pantomime. The music of Mozart has made it immortal and, blessedly, the music is all that matters on a CD recording; stagings vary from the sublime to the ridiculous.

We are asked to believe that my second choice above is 'the nearest to perfection one can expect in an imperfect world' (*Gramophone*, February 1994). This claim by Alan Blyth, who has studied his craft over a long lifetime, does not mean it is the recording to have if you have bought this book. It is what the perfectionist wants, but it takes a long time to appreciate finer things like original instruments. Academic accuracy was furthest from Mozart's mind when he wrote *The Magic Flute*. The alternative selections offer an all-star cast or a very fine recording at a third of the price of the other two!

| The Plot | The Queen of the Night asks Tamino to rescue her daughter Pamina from the clutches of the evil Sarastro, who turns out to be the benevolent guardian of a temple. Tamino and Pamina undergo three trials to test their character before being united.

MUSSORGSKY, Modest (1839–1881)

Boris Godounov ★ R d

(original) Kotcherga, Lipovšek, Wildhaber, Leiferkus, Ramey, BPO, Abbado
Sony S3K 58977 (3 CDs) $$$ DDD

(Rimsky-Korsakov) Ghiaurov, Vishnevskaya, Spiess, Maslennikov, Talvela, VPO, Karajan
Decca 411 862-2 (3 CDs) $$$ ADD

(Rimsky-Korsakov) Christoff, Zareska, Gedda, Borg, French Radio O, Dobrowen
EMI CHS5 65192-2 (mono) (3 CDs) $$ ADD

Mussorgsky

A huge, sombre and magnificent work, demanding a bass of overpowering personality for the title role, *Boris Godounov* has achieved almost a cult status. Attempting a production is a major event and people flock to it, though it is not a work for the newcomer to opera. The opportunities for spectacle are useless to the CD buyer, but consolations are many. Without the need to spend huge sums on elaborate scenery, all expenditure can go to engaging the best singers. Russia has always been famous for its basses and *Boris* is a Russian opera. The great Feodor Chaliapine brought it to the West for the first time at the beginning of this century and the greatest Borises ever since have come from Russia and Eastern Europe. Since the disintegration of the Soviet Union a huge number of superb singers previously unknown in the West have flooded our stages and *Boris* has been one of its greatest beneficiaries.

Mussorgsky never succeeded in putting a final version of the opera on stage and for decades an arrangement by Rimsky-Korsakov, which 'corrected Mussorgsky's mistakes' was the standard production seen and heard. Only one with Mussorgsky's original orchestration is recommendable over two Rimsky-Korsakov ones. In those, the major star of each generation is available on CD: Christoff in the fifties and Ghiaurov in the seventies. Christoff recorded Pimen and Varlaam as well as Boris, an interpretation which is probably as important as Chaliapine's would have been, had he only recorded it; the Christoff's continued existence in the catalogues in mono proves that, I think.

The Plot The new tsar Boris Godounov attained the throne by killing the legitimate heir, Dmitri, as a child. Grigory poses as the dead tsarevitch and rallies the people to support him. Conscience-stricken, Boris declines into madness and dies. Grigory and his followers set off for Moscow.

OFFENBACH, Jacques (1819–1880)

Les Contes d'Hoffmann (The Tales of Hoffmann) ★★★ R d

Sutherland, Tourangeau, Domingo, Bacquier, Suisse Romande O, Bonynge
Decca 417 363-2 (2 CDs) $$$ ADD
Highlights: **Decca 421 866-2 $$ ADD**

(Lind, Studer, Norman), Von Otter, Araiza, Ramey, Dresden Staatskapelle, Tate
Philips 422 374-2 (3 CDs) $$$ DDD
Highlights: **Philips 438 502-2 $$$ DDD**

(Serra, Norman, Plowright), Murray, Shicoff, Van Dam, Brussels Opera, Cambreling
EMI CDS7 49641-2 (2 CDs) $$$ DDD
Highlights: **EMI CDC7 54322-2 $$$ DDD**

Barcarolle • *Act 2 (s, ms)*
Doll Song • *Act 1 (s)*
Legend of Kleinsack • *Prologue (t)*
Scintille, diamant • *Act 2 (b)*

Offenbach never finished *The Tales of Hoffmann* and there is, therefore, no authentic complete version. There is, however, more than enough fine music to enable all kinds of different 'complete' versions to be staged. How they are made up is irrelevant. All the music is by Offenbach and all of it is good. On disc the visual aspects need not concern one, but with a prologue, epilogue and three acts, nothing goes on for too long and the composer manages to produce a variety of styles for each scene which are uniquely their own. Comedy, tragedy and high drama are all present under the same roof. No wonder the opera has had such continuing success.

The three main soprano parts are usually sung, as Offenbach intended, by one singer and Sutherland does just that in the cheapest set, with Domingo in the part he has sung more often than all others. The other two, quite legitimately, differentiate between the three characters, which are written, respectively, for coloratura, dramatic and lyric sopranos. Few singers can completely satisfy in all three spheres, though many have made a good stab at it. Araiza and Shicoff are fine Hoffmanns, if not as good as Domingo, and they have triple heroines, all good. The EMI set is the most complete, with Norman as Giulietta, not Antonia, as in the Philips. (NB: There are no recommendable CDs of Offenbach's two most popular operettas, *Orpheus in the Underworld* and *La belle Hélène*, on the market at present.)

The Plot The poet Hoffmann, drinking in a tavern, relates the tales of his three great loves, which then appear in the central acts: Olympia, the mechanical doll who comes to life through Hoffmann's rose-coloured spectacles; Giulietta, the Venetian courtesan, whose fate Offenbach left uncertain; and Antonia, the tubercular girl who is forbidden to sing, but forced to do so by the evil Dr Miracle, resulting in her death. Hoffmann drinks himself into forgetfulness in the epilogue.

PONCHIELLI, Amilcare (1834–1886)

La gioconda ★★ R d

Caballé, Baltsa, Pavarotti, Milnes, Ghiaurov, National PO, Bartoletti
Decca 414 349-2 (3 CDs) $$$ DDD

Callas, Cossotto, Ferraro, Cappuccilli, Vinco, La Scala Milan, Votto
EMI CDS7 49518-2 (3 CDs) $$$ ADD

Tebaldi, Horne, Bergonzi, Merrill, Ghiuselev, St Cecilia Rome O, Gardelli
Decca 430 042-2 (3 CDs) $$ ADD

Cielo e mar • Act 2 (t)
Suicidio! • Act 4 (s)
Enzo Grimaldo • Act 1 (t, b)
O monumento • Act 1 (b)

Ponchielli

The grandest of all the Italian grand operas, *La gioconda* has some of the most wonderful soaring tunes to be found in this field. Unfortunately, its sprawling, messy, incredibly convoluted plot can only be excused, or borne, by lovers of fine singing. My story synopsis cannot hope to do justice to even the basic plots, plural!

While a little subtlety does no harm here or there, the emphasis is on the strength (read loudness) of the singers. It must, of course, be accompanied by steadiness of voice and the old Callas set of 1959 shows the diva with a minimum of the unevenness, which even her greatest fans have to acknowledge. The Caballé set, however, has such a superb cast and better recording that it must be preferred by all but fanatic Callas admirers; but the same can be said of the older Tebaldi set, which is much cheaper.

| The Plot | Barnaba loves Gioconda, who loves Enzo, who loves Laura, who is married to Alvise, who orders Laura to take poison. With Gioconda's help, she does a Juliet by taking a death-simulating narcotic instead and escapes with Enzo. Barnaba thinks he has Gioconda, but she stabs herself rather than face a fate worse than death. Barnaba tells the dead woman that he has killed her mother. Why?

PORTER, Cole (1891–1964)

Kiss Me, Kate ★★★ M c

Barstow, Criswell, Hampson, London Sinfonia, McGlinn
EMI CDS7 54033-2 (2 CDs) $$$ DDD

P Morison, Kirk, Drake, original Broadway cast, Davenport
EMI ZDM7 64760-2 $$ ADD

Wunderbar • Act 1 (b, s)
So in Love • Act 1 (s)
Where is the life that late I led • Act 2 (b)
Brush up your Shakespeare • Act 2 (b, b)

The most successful of the seventeen operas based on Shakespeare's *The Taming of the Shrew*. It may have been a Broadway show but, like *Oklahoma!*°, which revolutionised the American musical theatre, *Kiss Me, Kate*'s music demands a full-sized baritone voice for the leading man. 'Wunderbar' is straight Strauss or

Lehár and the baritone's almost-patter songs need more than clarity of diction.

The full recording casts a famous Tosca and Leonore (Dame Josephine Barstow) opposite Thomas Hampson, a pair which commands respect in any opera house. The power of both principals is unmistakable and everybody's words are as clear as a bell. Like the EMI *Show Boat°* by Jerome Kern, this is a classic set. The original cast album offers only the principal numbers, but Morison and Drake made these under the supervision of Porter himself!

The Plot Long-term partners in show business, but now divorced, Fred and Lilli are appearing together in a production of *The Taming of the Shrew*. Fred is wooing Shakespeare's Bianca, not Kate, but Lilli gets his flowers by mistake and is suitably touched. In mid-performance she discovers the truth and suddenly becomes a real shrew. She walks out, leaving the rest of the cast and two un-Shakespearean gangsters to improvise. Yet, at the last moment, she reappears to eat humble pie by reading the Bard's final lines on stage.

PUCCINI, Giacomo (1858–1924)

La bohème ★★★ R d

De los Angeles, Amara, Björling, Merrill, RCA Victor O, Beecham
EMI CDS7 47235-2 (mono) (2 CDs) $$$ ADD

Freni, Harwood, Pavarotti, Panerai, BPO, Karajan
Decca 421 049-2 (2 CDs) $$$ ADD
Highlights: **Decca 421 245-2 $$$ ADD**

Tebaldi, d'Angelo, Bergonzi, Bastianini, St Cecilia Rome O, Serafin
Decca 421 301-2 (2 CDs) $$ ADD
Highlights: **Decca 421 301-2 $$ ADD**

Tebaldi, Gueden, Prandelli, Inghilleri, St Cecilia Rome O, Erede
Decca 440 233-2 (mono) (2 CDs) $$ ADD

Che gelida manina (Your tiny hand is frozen) • *Act 1 (t)*
Si, mi chiamano Mimì (They call me Mimì) • *Act 1 (s)*
O soave fanciulla (Lovely maid in the moonlight) • *Act 1 (t, s)*
Musetta's Waltz Song • *Act 2 (s)*

Puccini

The most popular Italian opera of them all and surely close to *Carmen°* in the universal stakes, *La bohème* is the ideal work to introduce anyone to this art form; it contains every type of vocal music, from the melodiously romantic to the brashly comic and the tragically sad. As happens too often, CDs reflect the absence of major stars in today's opera houses. The older singers were simply better than the new ones. The proof of that pudding lies in the fact that there is only one digital studio recording of this work and that is a second-rate bargain set; and of the seventeen available CD recordings, four are monaural!

Bohème was the vehicle which made Renata Tebaldi the biggest star before the arrival of Callas, whose mono recording (EMI CDS7 47475-2, 2 CDs, $$$ ADD) is also still in the catalogue. But Mimì was Tebaldi's role and her first recording of it is now on CD in a two-for-one bargain box, while her second is at medium price. Pavarotti fans will flock to his set, of course, but the best of them all remains the old De los Angeles/Björling recording, with Beecham really showing what Puccini wanted.

The Plot *Scènes de la vie de bohème* by Henri Mürger provided Puccini with the many characters, whose 'scenes' revolve around the poor poet Rodolfo and his love for the tubercular seamstress Mimì. Their poverty and her illness forces them to part, but she returns to his attic to die in his arms.

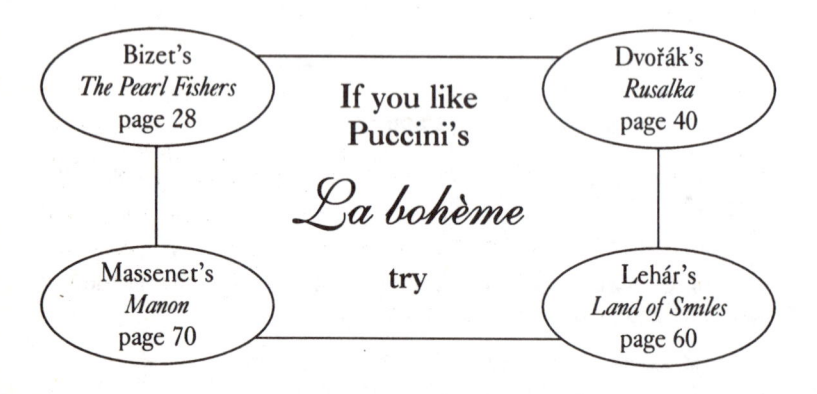

If you like Puccini's *La bohème* try:
- Bizet's *The Pearl Fishers* page 28
- Dvořák's *Rusalka* page 40
- Massenet's *Manon* page 70
- Lehár's *Land of Smiles* page 60

Puccini

La fanciulla del West (The Girl of the Golden West) ★ R d

Tebaldi, Del Monaco, MacNeil, St Cecilia Rome O, Capuana
Decca 421 595-2 $$ ADD

Neblett, Domingo, Milnes, CGO, Mehta
DG 419 640-2 $$$ ADD
Highlights: **DG 445 465-2 $$$ ADD**

Marton, O'Neill, Fondary, Munich Radio O, Slatkin
BMG/RCA 09026 60597 $$$ DDD

Ch'ella mi creda libero • Act 3 (t)
Laggiù nel Soledad • Act 1 (s)
Or son sei mesi • Act 2 (t)

The only genuine horse opera in the repertoire. Puccini's success was limited with this Italian work set in the Wild West, even though the 1910 première in the Metropolitan had Caruso as its tenor. The *Girl* quickly fell out of favour and was mainly remembered for the solitary aria listed first above. After World War II it began to be revived reasonably often and the complexity of the score began to be appreciated, even though it is a far cry from *La bohème°* or *Butterfly°*.

Again, the older singers score on available recordings. The DDD does not compare with the two earlier ones. The stentorian Del Monaco is, if anything, more suited to the music than the admirable Domingo, and Tebaldi has an edge over Neblett in anything by Puccini. But there is really very little to choose between them.

The Plot In a camp of Californian gold miners the hunted bandit Dick Johnson falls in love with Minnie, the owner of the local saloon, who has never been kissed! The Sheriff also wants Minnie, but is rejected. When Johnson is shot, she hides him in her loft. She and the Sheriff play cards, with Johnson's life and her body as the stakes, and she wins by cheating. When Johnson is captured by the miners, she reminds them of their loyalty to her and the united lovers set off into the sunset—on horseback in some theatres.

Puccini

Madama Butterfly ★★★ R d

Freni, Ludwig, Pavarotti, R Kerns, VPO, Karajan
Decca 417 577-2 (3 CDs) $$$ ADD
Highlights: **Decca 421 247-2 $$$ ADD**

Scotto, Di Stasio, Bergonzi, Panerai, Rome Opera, Barbirolli
EMI CMS7 63411-2 (2 CDs) $$ ADD
Highlights: **EMI 7 63411-2-653 $$$ ADD**

De los Angeles, Pirazzini, Björling, Sereni, Rome Opera, Santini
EMI CMS7 63634-2 (2 CDs) $$ ADD

Highlights (in English): Collier, Craig, Sadler's Wells O, Balkwill
Classics for Pleasure CD-CFP 4600 $ ADD

Un bel dì (One fine day) • Act 1 (s)
Love Duet • Act 1 (t, s)
Addio fiorito asil • Act 3 (t)
Flower Duet • Act 2 (s, ms)
Tu, tu, piccolo iddio! • Act 3 (s)

*T*his is a three-handkerchief tear-jerker, beloved of the ladies, God bless them, and Puccini's soaring melodies are really extremely hummable (including the 'Humming Chorus'!). They repeat themselves again and again—musically, you could condense *Butterfly* into half an hour without losing anything, but that does not alter the universal popularity of a work which, incredibly, was one of musical history's greatest disasters at its first performance in 1904; there was no second. The original was a two-act version, then revised by Puccini into three acts, in which form it was an instant success. It is this which is seen and recorded today, though the two-act original is occasionally revived with success (VSO, Melbourne 1994). This is not surprising, since it already contained all the above set pieces, except the short tenor aria. The locale in this case cannot be changed, only the period. Butterfly is Japanese and, though it is hard to hear the oriental overtones in such familiar music, they are certainly there. The central figure is on stage for all but a few minutes, while the tenor all but disappears after the first act. His importance in that is so great, however, that all the great tenors, from Caruso to the Three Tenors of our time, have all played Pinkerton.

There has never been one Butterfly greater than all others, but there are a lot of very fine ones on CD. Two conductors really dominate this scene: Karajan and Barbirolli. The former also conducts the old mono Callas set (EMI CDS7 47959-2 $$$ ADD), but Freni, Pavarotti and the recording in 1975 were at their very peak for him. Scotto has never been better than in the Barbirolli set, but there are at least four other CD sets which are close to the above. Personal preferences for favourite singers can safely influence your choice.

The Plot The American Lieutenant Pinkerton marries a Japanese girl in a casual fashion. She, Butterfly, believes that he really loves her and waits patiently with their son, of whom he knows nothing, for his return. When his ship finally comes back, he brings his American wife with him. Butterfly commits ceremonial suicide.

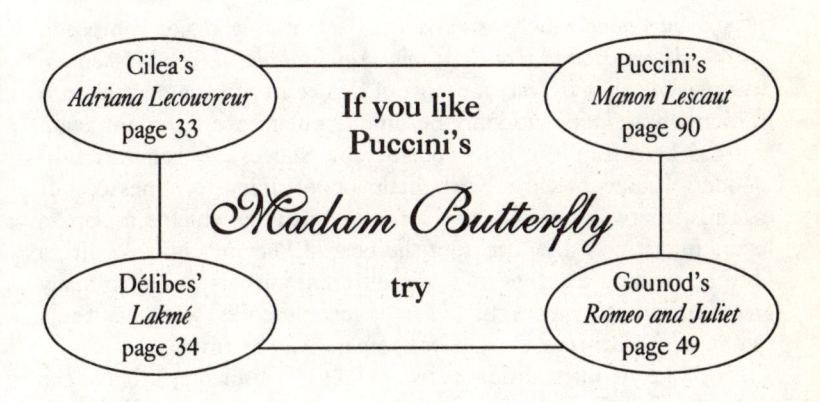

If you like Puccini's *Madam Butterfly* try

- Cilea's *Adriana Lecouvreur* page 33
- Puccini's *Manon Lescaut* page 90
- Délibes' *Lakmé* page 34
- Gounod's *Romeo and Juliet* page 49

Puccini

Manon Lescaut ★★ R d

Freni, Domingo, Bruson, CGO, Sinopoli
DG 413 893-2 (2 CDs) $$$ DDD
Highlights: **DG 445 466-2 $$ DDD**

Freni, Pavarotti, Croft, Metropolitan O, Levine
Decca 440 200-2 (2 CDs) $$$ DDD

Gauci, Kaludov, Sardinero, Brussels O, Rahbari
Naxos 8.660019/20 (2 CDs) $ DDD

Donna non vidi mai • *Act 1 (t)*
In quelle trine morbide • *Act 2 (s)*
Tu, tu, amore . . . O tentatrice • *Act 2 (t, s)*
Sola, perduta, abbandonata • *Act 4 (s)*

The opera which established Puccini as a major composer, *Manon Lescaut*, not to be mistaken for *Manon*° (see Massenet), was played solely in Italy for most of this century. It came back into fashion when opera suddenly became popular entertainment again and has held its place with considerable success. It requires full-blooded Italian bawling, with little opportunity for finesse, but extends the two principals to the full in a manner which most opera lovers find irresistible. Far from the best of Puccini's operas, with a libretto cobbled together by seven different authors, it has so many great arias and set pieces that it can be recommended wholeheartedly to non-cognoscenti in spite of its comparative obscurity.

There are many different recent CD sets available, a sign of the opera's popularity today. Freni partners both Domingo and Pavarotti, who is inclined to be on the loud side, no bad thing in this music, but Freni is better with Domingo. The extremely cheap Naxos set can be bought with confidence. It really is very good.

The Plot Young and innocent Manon is picked up by the impecunious Chevalier des Grieux. She leaves him in favour of a rich man, who lets her live in luxury. But her love for des Grieux draws them together again and her protector accuses her of prostitution. She is deported to Lousiana. Des Grieux goes with her, but she dies in misery while they are crossing a desert.

Puccini

La rondine ★★ R|

Te Kanawa, Domingo, Rendall, Nucci, LSO, Maazel
Sony M2K 37852 (2 CDs) $$ ADD

Moffo, Barioni, De Palma, Sereni, RCA Italian O, Molinari-Pradelli
BMG/RCA GD 60459 $$ ADD

Che il be sogno di Doretta • Act 1 (s)
Ore dolce e divine • Act 1 (s)

*O*nce curtly dismissed as rubbish, *La rondine* has established itself in recent years as a popular piece of lightweight Puccini, mainly through the appeal of the first aria listed above. Described as 'the poor man's *Traviata*', it started life as a Viennese operetta which was aborted by World War I, when Italy was on the side of the Allies. Its operetta image remains (including a glorious waltz while everybody drinks beer in romantic Paris!), but there is a touching final renunciation which indeed owes a debt to Verdi's opera.

Both recordings are fine; Kiri Te Kanawa is glorious and so is Domingo, though she is supposed to be much older than he and sounds decidedly younger. Moffo is one of the most unjustly neglected of sopranos, but Barioni is no match for Domingo.

|The Plot| A high-class courtesan, Magda, disguises herself as a grisette, visits a dance hall and falls in love with Ruggero. They live together. Ignorant of her past, he proposes marriage, but she decides it would ruin his life and leaves him.

Puccini

Tosca ★★★ R d

Callas, Di Stefano, Gobbi, La Scala Milan, De Sabata
EMI CDS7 47175-8 (mono) (2 CDs) $$$ ADD
Highlights: **EMI CDM7 64422-2 (mono) $$ ADD**

L Price, Di Stefano, Taddei, VPO, Karajan
Decca 421 670-2 (2 CDs) $$ ADD

Freni, Domingo, Ramey, CGO, Sinopoli
DG 431 775-2 (2 CDs) $$$ DDD
Highlights: **DG 437 547-2 $$$ DDD**

Highlights: Ricciarelli, Carreras, Raimondi, BPO, Karajan
DG 423 113-2 $$$ ADD

Highlights: Freni, Pavarotti, Milnes, National PO, Rescigno
Decca 421 888-2 $$ ADD

E lucevan le stelle (The stars were brightly shining) • Act 3 (t)
Vissi d'arte (Love and music) • Act 2 (s)
Recondita armonia (Strange harmony of contrasts) • Act 1 (t)
Tre sbirri • Act 1 (b, ch)

The famous quote that *Tosca* is a 'shabby little shocker' is only one-third true. It is not little and certainly not shabby, but it is a shocker, and a damned good one, too. Surprisingly, it has not surfaced as a straight film in this age of violence and sex—Puccini's music could very easily be used for the soundtrack. *Tosca* has everything going for it. It is short, to the point and does not linger at any time. From start to finish there is always something happening; only the famous arias temporarily halt the action and they are probably its greatest asset. Too strong for critics and public when it was first shown, it quickly became a perennial favourite and recordings of it abound.

Maria Callas recorded *Tosca* twice; the second version is best forgotten, but the first will almost certainly never be surpassed; and to hell with stereo or digital recordings. This is what opera is all about. Strangely, some of the best singers have left their mark on it more than once, and, unlike Callas, often bettering their performances. Giuseppe di Stefano appears twice in my short list, because he is partnered by other great singers and conductors. Mirella Freni has recorded it with both Domingo and Pavarotti, even though Tosca is not really her best part. Domingo and Samuel Ramey make mighty partners for her on the only digital recording among my recommendations. Leontyne Price and Giuseppe Taddei do well with Di Stefano before he went off the boil. The Ricciarelli/Carreras highlights are also fine, but Pavarotti has Freni before she reached her best as Tosca.

| The Plot | Scarpia, the police chief of Rome in the year 1800, lusts after Tosca. Her lover, Cavaradossi, assists an enemy of Scarpia to escape and is imprisoned and tortured. Tosca makes a deal with Scarpia, offering herself to him in exchange for Cavaradossi's freedom. After the deal is made, she kills Scarpia and hastens to Cavaradossi to tell him that his execution will be faked. It is not. Scarpia has his revenge after his death and Tosca leaps to her death.

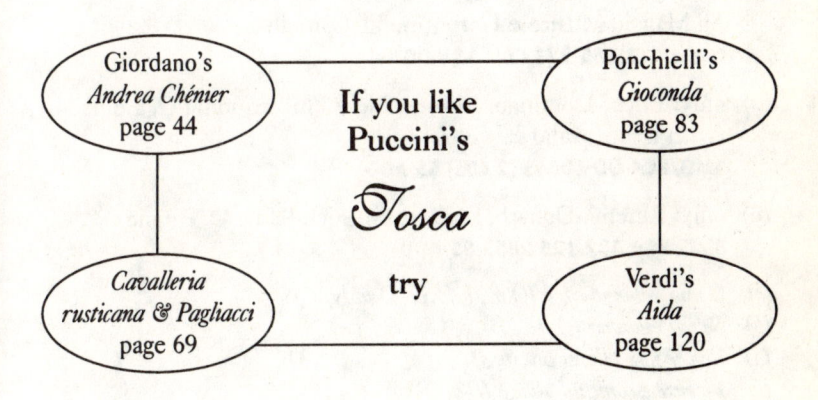

If you like Puccini's *Tosca* try

- Giordano's *Andrea Chénier* page 44
- Ponchielli's *Gioconda* page 83
- Cavalleria rusticana & Pagliacci page 69
- Verdi's *Aida* page 120

Il trittico ★★ R d & c

For a triple bill, *Il trittico* could really be no more varied. *Il tabarro* is Grand Guignol, blood and thunder à la *Tosca*°. *Suor Angelica*, Puccini's own favourite, is sugary sweetness with a miracle thrown in for good luck. *Gianni Schicchi* is high farce, almost slapstick. The three one-act operas, which made up a full evening of Puccini in 1918, are still usually shown together. They have, however, often been individually coupled with other works in the theatre. On disc there is only one (*Il tabarro*) partnered with another work, Leoncavallo's *Pagliacci*°.

Puccini

Il tabarro (a), Suor Angelica (b) and Gianni Schicchi (c)

- (a) Scotto, Domingo, Wixell, National PO, Maazel
- (b) Scotto, Horne, National PO, Maazel
- (c) Gobbi, Cotrubas, Domingo, LSO, Maazel
  Sony M3K 79312 (3 CDs) $$ ADD

- (a) Mas, Prandelli, Gobbi, Rome Opera, Bellezza (mono)
- (b) De los Angeles, Barbieri, Rome Opera, Serafin
- (c) Gobbi, De los Angeles, Del Monte, Rome Opera, Santini
  EMI CMS7 64165-2 (3 CDs) $$ ADD

- (a) Tebaldi, Del Monaco, Merrill
- (b) Tebaldi, Simionato
- (c) Corena, Tebaldi, Lazzari
  All Maggio Musicale Fiorentino O, Gardelli
  Decca 411 665-2 (3 CDs) $$ ADD

- (a) only: Price, Domingo, Milnes, New Philharmonia O, Leinsdorf
  (with Leoncavallo *Pagliacci*)
  BMG/RCA GD 60865 (2 CDs) $$ ADD

- (c) only: Panerai, Donath, Seiffert, Munich Radio O, Patané
  BMG/RCA 432 125 2852 $$ ADD

- (c) *O mio babbino caro (O my beloved Daddy) (s)*
- (b) *Senza mamma (s)*
- (a) *Perchè non m'ami più (b, s)*
- (c) *Firenze é come un albero (t)*
- (a) *Hai ben ragione (t)*

All three of the listed CD sets of the complete triple bill are older recordings. (There is a DDD Decca recording with Mirella Freni in the three soprano parts, but that cannot compete vocally.) The EMI was not even issued as a set originally, but has been put together for CD only recently. The most notable performer in two of the sets is Tito Gobbi; his second *Schicchi* was recorded twenty years after the first and is just as good! De los Angeles is sheer delight in (b) and (c) and Scotto does equally well in (a) and (b). Fedora Barbieri and Marilyn Horne are both excellent as the Princess in (b). The biggest attraction of *Il trittico* is, of course, 'O mio babbino caro' (Oh, my beloved daddy), the only famous tune in *Gianni Schicchi*. It may well be the masterpiece of the three, but it is farce as much as music, and visual characterisations are very much needed here. You can draw a parallel with Verdi's *Falstaff*° here; both are excellent comedies with brilliant musical backing, yet neither will ever win in the popularity stakes.

> The Plot (a) The barge master Michele suspects his wife of having an affair, but cannot fathom who her lover is. When the lover gives himself away, Michele promptly kills him, exposing his dead body to the wife under the cloak of the title.
> (b) Suor Angelica is a novice in a convent. She has had an illegitimate child and taken herself to a nunnery. There she is visited by the Princess, who informs her that the child has died. Angelica commits suicide, a mortal sin, but is forgiven through a miracle wrought by a statue of the Virgin Mary.
> (c) *Gianni Schicchi* is a farce about a will in which everything is left to the church. The heirs squabble among themselves and, finally, the confidence trickster Schicchi is asked for help. He impersonates the dead man and dictates a new will before independent witnesses in which a major part of the spoils goes to 'my good friend Gianni Schicchi'! The relatives can do nothing, but his daughter marries Rinuccio, a member of the family.

Turandot ★★★ C d

Sutherland, Caballé, Pavarotti, LPO, Mehta
Decca 414 274-2 (2 CDs) $$$ ADD
Highlights: **Decca 421 320-2 $$ ADD**

Nilsson, Scotto, Corelli, Rome Opera O, Molinari-Pradelli
EMI CMS7 69327-2 (2 CDs) $$$ ADD

Ricciarelli, Hendricks, Domingo, VPO, Karajan
DG 423 855-2 (2 CDs) $$$ DDD
Highlights: **DG 410 645-2 $$$ DDD**

Nessun dorma (None shall sleep) • *Act 3 (t)*
In questa reggia • *Act 2 (s)*
Tu che di gel • *Act 3 (s)*
Non piangere, Liù • *Act 1 (t)*
Signore ascolta • *Act 1 (s)*

Puccini

In spite of the many famous arias from *Turandot*, Puccini's last (and unfinished) opera is not an ideal work for the beginner. I have designated it 'C' (contemporary, twentieth century) because in it Puccini explored ways in music far removed from his early works and the gaps between the old melodious arias are not readily assimilated by the newcomer, who should buy CDs of highlights only. This in no way devaluates the work as a whole, but its failure to catch on internationally for thirty years after its 1926 première shows how slowly it was accepted.

Turandot certainly needs powerful Italian-type voices of fine quality and in the thirties and forties there was a shortage of these, as there is at present. Ricciarelli is really too light for the title role, except on disc, and Sutherland never sang the part on stage. Nevertheless, she sings it superbly and she does have Pavarotti in 'Nessun dorma' when he was at his very best. The older Nilsson/Corelli recording is also very fine and at mid-price!

| The Plot | The Princess Turandot hates men and her suitors have to forfeit their lives if they do not answer three riddles she sets. An unknown prince solves them, but allows Turandot to avoid marriage if she can discover his name by the next morning, hence 'none shall sleep' in Peking, but none finds the name either. Inevitably, the icy Turandot melts and falls for the now identified Calaf.

RODGERS, Richard (1902–1979)
& Oscar Hammerstein II (1895–1960)

The King and I ★★★ M1

Andrews, Horne, Kingsley, Hollywood Bowl O, Mauceri
Philips 438 007-2 $$$ DDD

Nixon (for Deborah Kerr), Brynner, film soundtrack, Newman
EMI ZDM7 64693-2 $$ ADD

Cook, Scovotti, Bikel, Broadway cast
Sony SK 53328 $$ ADD

Shall we dance? • Act 2 (s, b)
Hello, young lovers • Act 1 (s)
I whistle a happy tune • Act 1 (s)
Getting to know you • Act 1 (s, ch)

The collaboration of Richard Rodgers with Oscar Hammerstein II (his grandfather was the only serious competitor the Metropolitan Opera House in New York ever had) produced a series of Broadway musicals which revolutionised the genre; many of their works have been in the repertoire of opera houses for years by now. Their works are rightly known as Rodgers and Hammerstein, like Gilbert and Sullivan, though Rodgers is listed before the librettist, unlike G & S, because he had a long and glorious career earlier with Lorenz Hart. (Their work together was somewhat less operatic in character.) The musical-cum-operas of R & H can only be described as 'having heart'. However sentimental their tales may appear to some, each of their works is a dramatic entity into which the songs flow naturally as part of the action. Their only predecessor in this respect was *Showboat°*, which has become equally immortal. *The King and I* is a typical example, able to bring tears at its end as much as *La bohème°* can.

Julie Andrews makes an astonishingly effective Anna no fewer than thirty-six years after playing Eliza in *My Fair Lady°* and the great actor Ben Kingsley is a fine King. Marilyn Horne sings her solitary song beautifully. The original King, Yul Brynner, made a lifetime career out of playing the totally bald King, but on disc his personal magnetism only carries for people who have seen the film. Paradoxically, Marni Nixon provided the voice not only for Anna, but for the Julie Andrews part in the film of *My Fair Lady*. I have not heard the Barbara Cook/Theodore Bikel recording, but Anna was Cook's favourite part and Cook is the only American musical star as good as Julie Andrews.

The Plot The King of Siam engages the English widow, Anna, to educate his children. Initially there is a tremendous clash of cultures and the physical attraction between the two is totally suppressed throughout, while the King gradually accepts tolerance in place of totalitarianism for the Crown Prince's future role. The King dies, of course, and democracy of a kind will rule in future. Hurrah!

Oklahoma! ★★★ M l

S Jones, MacRae, film soundtrack, Blackton
EMI ZDM7 64691-2 $$ ADD

Haskins, Eddy, O, Engel
Sony SK 53326 mono $$$ ADD

Andreas, Guittard, 1980 Broadway cast, Blackton
RCA RD 83572 $$ ADD

Oh, what a beautiful morning • *Act 1 (b)*
Out of my dreams • *Act 2 (b, s)*
The surrey with the fringe on top • *Act 1 (b)*
People will say we're in love • *Act 1 (b, s)*

The musical which pioneered a new art form and which even has a truly operatic story, with a fully fledged dramatic baritone villain and a major ballet sequence. *Oklahoma!* is valid music drama just as much as Puccini's *Tosca°*, though the music is lighter and there is a fair amount of comedy involved. The music really demands operatic voices; there were no microphones in those early musicals and the American ranch setting at the turn of the century is more convincing than that of Puccini's *The Girl of the Golden West°*. Two of the CDs are old, the soundtrack dating from 1955 and the Nelson Eddy even earlier—the old partner of Jeannette MacDonald is in fine voice. The 1980 Broadway version is probably the most polished.

The Plot The cowhand Curly loves Laurey, but the rough hired hand, Jud, tries to court Laurey with such crudeness that she fires him. After the wedding of Laurey and Curly, Jud turns up with a knife seeking revenge, but accidentally kills himself instead. The local judge is convinced by the community that Curly is no murderer, as indeed he is not.

The Sound of Music ★★★ M d

Martin, Bikel, Neway, original Broadway cast, Dvonch
Sony SK 53537 $$ ADD

Andrews, McKay (for Peggy Wood), Plummer, film soundtrack, Kostal
BMG/RCA ND 90368 $$ ADD

The Sound of Music • Act 1 (s)
Edelweiss • Act 1 (s, b)
Climb every mountain • Act 2 (ms)
My favourite things • Act 1 (s)
Do-re-mi • Act 1 (s)

There can never have been a greater perennial than *The Sound of Music*; on stage and on film it has had record runs over the years and it is still revived at regular intervals. The film has identified it with Julie Andrews, but the stage production of 1959 starred Mary Martin, who had also launched *South Pacific*° ten years earlier. It is Andrews and her clear diction, which allows every word to be understood, who makes this such an enjoyable experience. Unlike *South Pacific*, there is only one hit song which does not belong to the leading lady, and that, contrary to the record notes, is not sung by the Australian singer who acted the Mother Abbess, Peggy Wood, but is the dubbed voice of one Margery McKay. In the original cast recording 'Climb every mountain' is sung by Patricia Neway, the first Magda in Menotti's *The Consul*. The plot, based on the real-life experiences of the Von Trapp family, was more topical in 1959 than it is today, but escaping from tyranny is never out of date, making this very much a dramatic musical-cum-opera.

|The Plot| The Austrian Baron von Trapp acquires a young novice from a local nunnery as a governess to his seven motherless children. They fall in love and marry, but are forced to flee from the incoming Nazis; with success, of course.

South Pacific ★★★ M1

Martin, Hall, Pinza, Tabbert, original Broadway cast, Dell'Isola
Sony SK 53327 (mono) $$$ ADD

Gaynor, M Smith (for Hall), Tozzi (for Rossano Brazzi), B Lee (for John Kerr), film soundtrack, Newman
BMG/RCA ND 83681 $$ ADD

Te Kanawa, Carreras, Patinkin, Vaughan
Sony 42205 $$ DDD

Some enchanted evening • Act 1 (ba)
A wonderful guy • Act 1 (s)
Younger than springtime • Act 1 (t)
Bali Ha'i • Act 1 (ms)

The success of *South Pacific* was largely based on the spectacular performance of the elderly but still handsome bass from the Metropolitan, Ezio Pinza. The voice of Giorgio Tozzi, his successor at the Met, was used in the film, while the romantic Italian Rossano Brazzi acted the part. Clearly, this show needs a major bass to sing the music. As for Mary Martin, she had a good soprano voice, though she was too attractive ever to leave Broadway musicals. Together they made the Rodgers and Hammerstein show a roaring success. Juanita Hall's Polynesian mammy, Bloody Mary, belonged as much to the negro stereotype as to any genuine Hawaiian, but 'Bali Ha'i' was a hit both on Broadway and in Hollywood. There is nothing wrong with the film soundtrack, but Pinza and Martin are the genuine article, though only reproduced in monaural sound. The Te Kanawa/Carreras recording is strictly for their fans alone.

The Plot A South Pacific island during World War II. Emile de Becque, a French planter with two Eurasian children, falls in love with American nurse Nellie Forbush. He goes off to war. On returning, he finds that she has been caring for his children and they marry.

ROMBERG, Sigmund (1887–1951)

The Student Prince ★★★ R I

Hill Smith, Ashe, Rendall, Bailey, Bottone, Philharmonia O, Edwards
TER CDTER 1172 (2 CDs) $$$ DDD

Blyth, Lanza, film soundtrack, Callinicos
BMG/RCA GD 60889 $$$ ADD

The Drinking Song • Act 1 (t)
Deep in my heart • Act 1 (t, s)
Overhead the moon is beaming • Act 1 (t)
Golden days • Act 1 (b)

This is the only old-fashioned Ruritania-type musical in English to survive in CD form. Lanza fans will obviously opt for his recording of the film in which only his voice was seen/heard. The complete set, with major British singers in leading roles, makes for good entertainment, if Romberg is your cup of tea. This is complete, not only including all the standard pops, but also the important final scene.

The Plot Prince Karl-Franz falls in love with the waitress Kathie while attending Heidelberg university as a student. When his father dies he becomes king and is supposed to marry a princess. Unusually, the princess visits Kathie and they both agree that it is best for Karl-Franz to marry his consort, leaving Kathie with only memories.

Rossini

ROSSINI, Gioacchino (1792–1868)

Il barbiere di Siviglia (The Barber of Seville) ★★★ R c

Bartoli, Matteuzzi, Nucci, Burchuladze, Bologna Opera, Patané
Decca 425 520-2 (3 CDs) $$$ DDD
Highlights: **Decca 440 289-2 $$$ DDD**

Mentzer, Hadley, Hampson, Ramey, Toscana O, Gelmetti
EMI CDS7 54863-2 (3 CDs) $$$ DDD

Ganassi, Vargas, Servile, de Grandis, CO Budapest, Humburg
Naxos 8.66027/9 (3 CDs) $ DDD

Highlights: Callas, Alva, Gobbi, Philharmonia O, Galliera
EMI CDM7 63076-2 $$ ADD

Largo al factotum • *Act 1 (b)*
Una voce poco fa • *Act 1 (s)*
Ecco ridente • *Act 1 (t)*
La calunnia • *Act 1 (ba)*
Dunque io son • *Act 1 (s, b)*

With no less than three new recordings in 1994—and others probably on the way—there are so many fine versions that I cannot restrict myself solely to the above three, which are excellent and have the most modern sound, yet are not way ahead of the ones I will mention below. *The Barber* is by far the most successful comic opera ever written, but an understanding of the complex plot in detail is essential. (Get that libretto out and double your enjoyment.)

Incredibly, all the best recordings are the most recent ones, for once. With Cecilia Bartoli the outstanding box office draw of today, her Rosina probably has most appeal. The EMI recording has a better all-round cast. The Naxos is an outstandingly lively performance with comparative unknowns in the cast, but costs a third of the other two. The advantages of all three are offset by two two-disc versions, a new one with the magnificent Jennifer Larmore, Håkan Hagegård, Raúl Giménez and Samuel Ramey (Teldec 9031-74885-2 $$$ DDD) and the old one with Callas (EMI CDS7 47634-8 $$$ ADD). It is also worth mentioning the DG 1992 set, also on two CDs, which stars Domingo as the baritone Figaro! And he is better than his colleagues Kathleen Battle and Ruggero Raimondi, while Frank Lopardo makes a fine Almaviva (DG 435 763-2 $$$ DDD). Make of that lot what you will. I know of no other opera with has so many acceptable alternatives on CD.

The Plot The Count Almaviva is courting Rosina, who is kept under lock and key by her guardian, who wants to marry her himself. With the help of Figaro, Almaviva enters their house illegally three times, twice in disguise, and marries Rosina, allowing the guardian to keep the money, which is all he wants anyway. (The plot continues in Mozart's *Marriage of Figaro°*.)

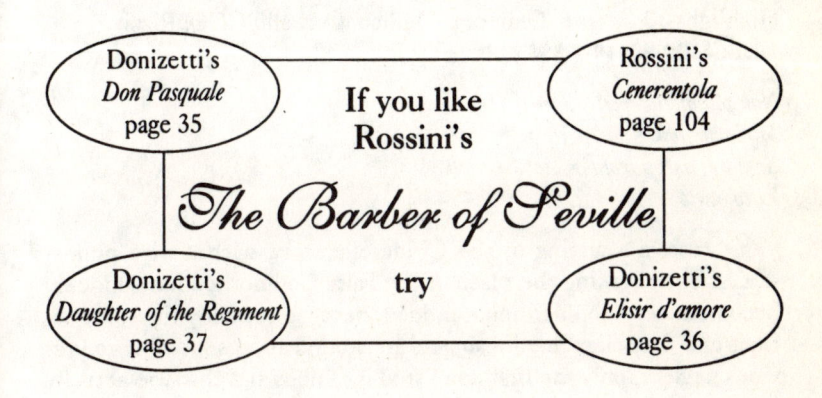

If you like Rossini's *The Barber of Seville* try

- Donizetti's *Don Pasquale* page 35
- Rossini's *Cenerentola* page 104
- Donizetti's *Daughter of the Regiment* page 37
- Donizetti's *Elisir d'amore* page 36

Rossini

La Cenerentola (Cinderella) ★★★ R c

Bartoli, Mateuzzi, Corbelli, Dara, Bologna O, Chailly
Decca 436 902-2-2 (2 CDs) $$$ DDD
Highlights: **Decca 444 183-2 $$$ DDD**

Baltsa, Araiza, Alaimo, Raimondi, ASMF, Marriner
Philips 420 468-2 (2 CDs) $$$ DDD

Gabarain, Oncina, Bruscantini, Glyndebourne O, Gui
EMI CMS7 64183-2 (mono) (2 CDs) $$ ADD

Highlights: Larmore, Giménez, Quilico, Corbelli, CGO, Rizzi
Teldec 4509-98819-2 $$$ DDD

Non più mesta • *Act 2 (ms)*
Miei rampoli • *Act 1 (ba)*
Signore, una parola • *Act 1 (ms, ba)*
Zitto, zitto • *Act 1 (t, b)*

Rossini's setting of the Cinderella story, with a wise philosopher taking the place of the Fairy Godmother, has suddenly become a very popular opera indeed, because so many fine productions and first-class Rossini singers are around at present. Due to previous neglect, only the first aria listed is famous and that was actually transferred from *The Barber of Seville*°, where it was originally sung by the tenor. There is no glass slipper or magic in this version, nor are the sisters necessarily ugly. The music is exceptionally tuneful and the plot easy enough to follow.

All three versions listed are as good as anything you can get in the theatre. Cecilia Bartoli is the great name today, thanks to worldwide promotion by Decca Records. Her partners are admirable and hers is also the best recording. But there is nothing wrong with the Philips, and the Glyndebourne monaural set is a classic which still sells forty-two years after it was made.

The Plot Prince Ramiro exchanges identity with his valet, Dandini, to judge the merits of Don Magnifico's daughters with a view to marriage. Cenerentola (Cinderella) is not in the running, but her sisters fawn on the false Prince, while he and Cinderella fall in love. Ramiro's tutor invites Cinderella to the ball and provides her with a suitable gown. There is no leave-taking at midnight, but half a bracelet proves to the Prince that the unknown beauty is the skivvy he met in Magnifico's castle.

Semiramide ★★ R d

Studer, Larmore, Lopardo, Ramey, LSO, Marin
DG 437 797-2 (3 CDs) $$$ DDD
Highlights: **DG 437 813-2 $$$ DDD**

Sutherland, Horne, Serge, Rouleau, LSO, Bonynge
Decca 425 481-2 $$ ADD

Bel raggio lusinghier • Act 1 (s)
Serbami ognor • Act 1 (s, ms)
Eccomi alfine • Act 1 (ms)
Ah! la sorte ci tradi • Act 2 (ba)

*A*n opera famous largely for an aria which every coloratura soprano wants to sing, yet few do. But for the appearance of Joan Sutherland, it is likely that *Semiramide* would be as unknown as the many other serious Rossini operas. The combination of Sutherland and Marilyn Horne during the seventies suddenly put it very much on the map and the remarkable achievement of Cheryl Studer in tackling the title role, after successfully recording the very different *Salome*°, has ensured the continued interest of a public eager for such bel canto operas, in which the singing is all that matters. The libretto is a farrago of nonsense, but Rossini's music is melodious from start to finish and with two such leading ladies either set is well worth acquiring. Sutherland and Horne are probably unbeatable, but Studer's supporting cast is much better and she also has digital sound. The tenor's comparatively small role is enlarged in the much fuller Studer set and Ramey is truly superb in one of the longest and most difficult bass roles in Italian opera. Yet, who would want to do without Sutherland and Horne? (Note: the part of Arsace is sung by the mezzo-soprano.)

The Plot Queen Semiramide and Prince Assur have killed her husband, Nino. A successor has to be named. Semiramide is in love with the army commander Arsace who, unknown to her, is her own son! The gods don't like this and Nino's ghost demands that Arsace avenge his murder. Assur wants to be king, but the succession is complicated by the fact that Semiramide as well as Arsace have become aware of their relationship and the gods demand a human sacrifice. Assur tries to kill Arsace. Semiramide wants to kill Assur. Arsace accidentally kills Semiramide instead of Assur, who is arrested, while Arsace becomes king. Don't ask me why. Ask Rossini.

SAINT-SAËNS, Camille (1835–1921)

Samson and Delilah ★★ R d

Meier, Domingo, Fondary, Bastille Opera, Chung
EMI CDS7 54470-2 (2 CDs) $$$ DDD

Gorr, Vickers, Blanc, Paris Opéra, Prêtre
EMI CDS7 47895-2 (2 CDs) $$$ ADD
Highlights: **EMI CDM7 63935-2 $$ ADD**

Baltsa, Carreras, Summers, Bavarian Radio SO, Davis
Philips 426 243-2 (2 CDs) $$$ DDD
Highlights: **Philips 438 504-2 $$$ DDD**

Mon coeur s'ouvre (Softly awakes my heart) • Act 2 (ms)
Amour, viens aider • Act 2 (ms)
Printemps qui commence • Act 1 (ms)

The great role for a mezzo-soprano or the old-fashioned contralto voice, Delilah has to compete with an equally compelling tenor Samson, for whom Saint-Saëns forgot to write any decent arias. The three great set pieces have been recorded endlessly and the rest of the opera is very much in keeping with the feeling they engender. This is a biblical spectacle, but it is the music which counts on CD and that is highly dramatic in a more continuous manner than was customary in Italian opera in the 1860s, when it was composed. Biblical subjects not being allowed on the Victorian stage, England did not see *Samson and Delilah* until 1909. It is interesting to note that the text of the libretto never reveals what it is that brings about Samson's downfall.

Jon Vickers is the best Samson and Rita Gorr even more easily outshines both her rivals, but the recording and the supporting cast led by Georges Prêtre let them down. All three sets are curate's eggs, with the good outweighing the bad. In the modern sets Meier is much better than Baltsa, but her Samson, Carreras, is not as strong as Baltsa's Domingo.

The Plot Samson is the phenomenally strong leader of the Israelites. The Philistine Delilah seduces him and obtains the secret of his strength, which lies in his hair. Delilah gives him a haircut while he is asleep, and he is captured and blinded. Samson prays to God for a return of his strength and brings down the heathen temple, crushing all within it.

THE TOP TEN
Mezzo-sopranos in Operas
ON CD

Agnes BALTSA
Fedora BARBIERI
Cecilia BARTOLI
Grace BUMBRY
Fiorenza COSSOTTO
Brigitte FASSBAENDER
Marilyn HORNE
Jennifer LARMORE
Christa LUDWIG
Shirley VERRETT

Smetana

SMETANA, Bedřich (1824–1884)

The Bartered Bride ★★★ R1

Beňačková, Dvorsky, Kopp, Novák, Czech PO, Košler
Supraphon 10 3511-2 (3 CDs) $$$ DDD
Highlights: **Supraphon 1122512 $$$ ADD**

(in German) Lorengar, Wunderlich, Frick, Bamberg SO, Kempe
EMI CMS7 64002-2 (2 CDs) $$ ADD
Highlights: **EMI 7 60094-2-555 $$$ ADD**

(in German) Stratas, Kollo, Berry, Munich Radio O, Krombholc
BMG/Eurodisc 352887 (2 CDs) $$ ADD

How could they believe • Act 2 (t)
The dream of love • Act 3 (s)
I know a girl • Act 2 (t, ba)
Mařenka–Jeník duet • Act 3 (t, s)

For most of this century *The Bartered Bride* was usually performed in German outside Czechoslovakia and its arias gained immense popularity in that language, in spite of the fact that there were always many more recordings in Czech. The original language trend in recent years has resulted in the performance of Slavonic operas in the original Czech, Russian or Hungarian, as the case may be. What matters to us, however, is the music, which is an ideal blend of charm, romance, comedy and whimsy. Many of its orchestral highlights are standard classical pops.

It would be hard to have it sung better than on the three CD sets now available. Beňačková is a superb artist with a most beautiful voice and Dvorsky has sung the main operatic repertoire in the world's greatest theatres. The two German versions are equally good, the older (Lorengar/Wunderlich) possibly having the edge. Yet Stratas and Kollo are as good as they come today.

<u>The Plot</u> Mařenka's father has promised her hand to the son of Micha, Vašek, but she loves Jeník, who has a mysterious past. In return for a sum of money, Kecal and Jeník agree that Mařenka will marry the son of Micha. It turns out that Jeník is Micha's son from an earlier marriage and the young couple get a handsome dowry from the unhappy Kecal.

STRAUSS, Johann, Jr (1825-1899)

Die Fledermaus ★★★ R c

Te Kanawa, Gruberová, Brendel, Leech, Bär, Fassbaender, VPO, Previn
Philips 432 157-2 (2 CDs) $$$ DDD
Highlights: **Philips 438 503-2 $$$ DDD**

Schwarzkopf, Streich, Gedda, Krebs, Kunz, Christ, Philharmonia O, Karajan
EMI CHS7 69531-2 (mono) (2 CDs) $$ ADD

Popp, Lind, Seiffert, Domingo, Brendel, Bavarian Radio O, Domingo
EMI 7 47480-2 (2 CDs) $$$ DDD
Highlights: **EMI 7 49866-2 $$$ DDD**

Mein Herr Marquis (Laughing Song) • *Act 2 (s)*
Klänge der Heimat (Csárdás) • *Act 2 (s)*
Trinke Liebchen • *Act 1 (t or b, s)*
Herr Chevalier, Finale • *Act 2 (t or b, s, ch)*

The first operetta in history which was accepted as a fully fledged opera, Johann Strauss' masterpiece is vastly superior to any of his other stage works, most of which have not lasted the distance, even though each contains delightful music. Many Strauss waltzes are immortal and *Die Fledermaus* has its fair share of them. Nevertheless, it is the truly operatic integration of music and plot which makes this work such a delight. It may be a ridiculous simile, but Strauss embodies the principles of Gluck in this piece of froth; the music totally reflects the words, which enact one of the most delightful of comedies ever produced by anyone. Strauss' music lifts it far above the gross French farce on which it is based; the plot hardly stands the test of logical dramaturgy.

Purists may prefer the charm of Karajan's old mono set with Schwarzkopf & Co, including the best singers of the fifties, but Previn's digital recording is musically and vocally as good as anything which is likely to appear in the foreseeable future. The double-Domingo set (he sings Alfred and conducts as well!) is not bad at all either.

Strauss

The Plot Eisenstein has been sentenced to five days in prison for a minor offence. He, his wife Rosalinde, his maid Adele, his friend Dr Falke and even Frank, the governor of the gaol, are all determined to attend a ball at the palace of Prince Orlovsky, one and all disguised as something they are not. Things get complicated when Rosalinde is visited by Alfred, an old flame, after Eisenstein has departed for the ball. When Frank arrives to take Eisenstein to gaol, Alfred takes his place. Thus when Eisenstein presents himself to serve his sentence in the morning, he finds that he is already behind bars! The resolution is ingenious and logical in purely Viennese fashion.

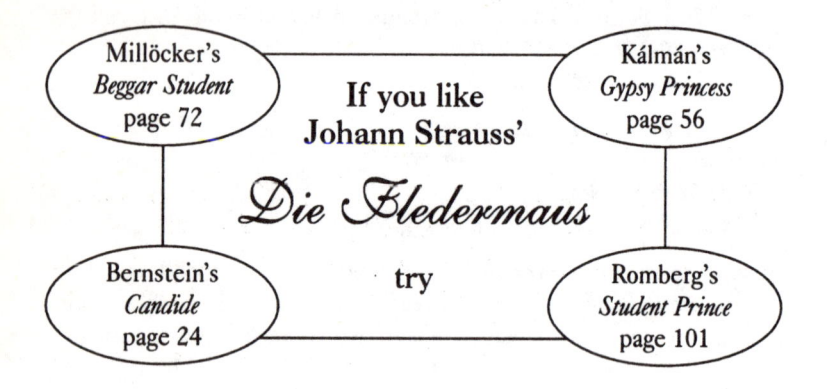

If you like Johann Strauss'

Die Fledermaus

try

- Millöcker's *Beggar Student* page 72
- Kálmán's *Gypsy Princess* page 56
- Bernstein's *Candide* page 24
- Romberg's *Student Prince* page 101

Der Zigeunerbaron (The Gypsy Baron) ★★★ R l

Schwarzkopf, Gedda, Kunz, Prey, Philharmonia O, Ackermann
EMI CHS7 69526-2 (mono) (2 CDs) $$$ ADD

Lindner, Protschka, Gramatzki, Fischer-Dieskau, Munich Radio O, Boskovsky
EMI 7 49231-2-667 (2 CDs) $$$ ADD

Coburn, Hamari, Lippert, Schasching, Vienna SO, Harnoncourt
Teldec 4509-94555-2 (2 CDs) $$$ DDD

Highlights: Schädle, Schock, Kusche, Deutsche Oper Berlin, Stolz
BMG/Eurodisc 258368 $$ ADD

Als flotter Geist (Open Road) • Act 1 (t)
Wer uns getraut • Act 2 (t, s)
So elend und treu • Act 1 (s)
Ja das Schreiben und das Lesen • Act 1 (b)

The closest Johann Strauss ever came to writing a proper opera, *The Gypsy Baron* has some truly operatic moments in it and can only be sung by full-sized voices. The Hungarian (read: gypsy) element is very strong, but the work is seldom heard outside German-speaking countries, in spite of its many famous arias.

The classic Schwarzkopf/Gedda/Kunz/Prey combination is unlikely ever to be bettered, but Boskovsky is the century's best Strauss conductor, and his cast is fine. The 1995 Teldec recording is the most complete, with all the traditional cuts (a claimed 40 minutes of music!) restored by, of all things, a baroque music specialist, Nikolaus Harnoncourt. The unfamiliar cast is headed by a Covent Garden Tamino, Herbert Lippert, who has also recorded *The Magic Flute*°. (There is no recording of the version still occasionally televised, in which the tenor is Bayreuth's Wagnerian Siegfried Jerusalem, who was billed as Siegfried Salem, his real names considered to be a strange coupling for a German at first.)

The Plot The self-proclaimed 'Gypsy Baron' Barinkay wants to marry Sáffi, but finds that she is of noble birth and he is, after all, a commoner. So, he joins the army instead. Coming back as a hero, he is made a real baron by the emperor and can now marry his aristocratic girlfriend.

STRAUSS, Richard (1864–1949)

Der Rosenkavalier ★★ C |

Schwarzkopf, Ludwig, Stich-Randall, Edelmann, Philharmonia O, Karajan
EMI CDS7 49354-2 (3 CDs) $$$ ADD
Highlights: **EMI CDM7 63452-2 $$ ADD**

Te Kanawa, Von Otter, Hendricks, Rydl, Dresden Staatskapelle, Haitink
EMI CDS7 54259-2 (3 CDs) $$$ DDD
Highlights: **EMI 7 54493-2 $$$ DDD**

Crespin, Donath, Minton, Jungwirth, VPO, Solti
Decca 417 493-2 (3 CDs) $$$ ADD

Herr Kavalier • Act 2 (ba)
Mir ist die Ehre (Presentation of the silver rose) • Act 2 (ms, s)
Di rigori amato • Act 1 (t)
Ist ein Traum • Act 3 (ms, s)

Der Rosenkavalier requires a degree of intelligence to appreciate to the full its many beauties, its wit and its psychological insights. There are plenty of conventional melodies, including a set of waltzes which are, like the text, deliberately fake Viennese. Yet the highlights of the score lie elsewhere, in the sublime 'Presentation of the Silver Rose' and the final duet of the lovers. Strauss and his librettist, Hugo von Hofmannsthal, invented a mythical eighteenth-century Vienna in which is played out an old-fashioned farce à la Molière. There is a subplot which, musically, is a most important part of the score; the leading lady, the Marschallin, could be removed from the story line without affecting it. She is an aging ('no more than thirty-two', according to Strauss) woman whose lover is the teen-aged Octavian of the title. Her reflections on life passing her by have no bearing on the story itself and the character was only a late addition to the score.

    Rosenkavalier has had a good run on CD. I have omitted two good ones only because of the comparative weakness of the Marschallin; Anna Tomova-Sintow cannot compete with Schwarzkopf, Te Kanawa or Crespin, although she has the best Baron Ochs in Kurt Moll (DG

423 850-2, 3 CDs, $$$ DDD) and Maria Reining is really inadequate in an otherwise superlative cast in the otherwise wonderful old Erich Kleiber recording (Decca 425 950-2, mono, 3 CDs, $$ ADD). The Solti set has a fine Marschallin in Régine Crespin, a superb Octavian in Yvonne Minton and a good cast, but the transfer to CD is not good enough to justify the full price when the Schwarzkopf one is cheaper and Te Kanawa has better sound.

|The Plot| Octavian, the young lover of the aging Marschallin, is sent by the bumptious Baron Ochs as go-between to propose marriage to Sophie. Octavian and Sophie fall in love and arrange to expose Ochs to public ridicule. Octavian disguises himself as a girl and Ochs promptly tries to seduce her/him. The Marschallin gives up Octavian to the younger woman.

Salome ★ C d

Studer, Rysanek, Hiestermann, Terfel, Deutsche Oper Berlin, Sinopoli
DG 431 810-2 (2 CDs) $$$ DDD

Norman, Witt, Raffeiner, Morris, Dresden Staatskapelle, Ozawa
Philips 432 153-2 (2 CDs) $$$ DDD

Behrends, Baltsa, K-W Böhm, Van Dam, VPO, Karajan
EMI CDS7 49358-2 (2 CDs) $$$ DDD

Ach, ich habe deinen Mund geküsst (s)

The most recent recordings of *Salome* are the best ones, because it relies tremendously on its huge orchestra and none of the historic singers of the past have left a lasting impression in the hefty title role. This strange hybrid—a French play by an English playwright (Oscar Wilde) translated into German—features remarkable and unprecedented examples of horrendous psychiatrically evil creatures too real for comfort. Wilde's original *Salome* barely survives, but the music of Strauss has kept it in the public eye, and the many films about Salome are usually reflections of the opera rather than the play.

The glory on CD is shared between the soprano and the conductor. Studer and Sinopoli are the ideal combination. Jessye Norman outshines Ozawa, and Karajan adds more to his set than Behrends. Yet all three ladies give performances which, by rights, should only happen once in a generation. There is even a fourth partnership close behind: Birgit Nilsson and Georg Solti (Decca 414 414-2, 2 CDs, $$$ ADD). *Salome* is not an opera for the faint-hearted, nor is it tuneful in the accepted sense. It is musical theatre at its best.

> The Plot The very young Salome lusts after John, the Baptist. Her stepfather, Herod, lusts after her. The Baptist rejects Salome and she demands his head before she will drop her seven veils while dancing for Herod. What she does with the Baptist's severed head is so disgusting to even this depraved spectator that he orders that she be killed.

SULLIVAN, Arthur (1842–1900)

The many popular Gilbert and Sullivan operas, or operettas, were written so much to formula that it is almost pointless to write about them individually. Every one has the same kind of tenor and the same kind of hefty contralto, though today they call themselves mezzo-sopranos. And each has a comic lead of indeterminate voice type, usually baritone. Gilbert was the master, not the servant of the music and Sullivan strongly objected to playing second fiddle to him. While the music may be the most important part of buying G & S on CD, the words cannot and should not be ignored. The sad and glad reality is that there is little to choose between the music of the various works. Even the least important are tuneful and only one, *The Yeomen of the Guard*, has any kind of serious subject.

None of the Gilbertian plots can be summarised briefly; their very complexity is their strength. I am therefore grouping recordings into two classes: those with spoken dialogue and those without. The days when G & S was controlled by the D'Oyly Carte family have long gone, fortunately; their musical standards would not pass today. English becoming the universal language, many of the operas are in the catalogues in other countries, in their original English, just as we in turn produce their works in their languages. There are two good classic sets:

- The Decca D'Oyly Carte from the sixties, which are true to tradition in all but singing and recording standards, which are much better than in the past. Their principals usually feature John Reed in the comic roles and a variety of good sopranos, tenors etc., conducted by Isadore Godfrey.

- The other classic sets on EMI are conducted by Sir Malcolm Sargent and use major British opera singers like Elsie Morison, Richard Lewis and Geraint Evans, with the comic roles taken by the aging, but still brilliant George Baker.

These older sets are very good indeed, but more recent (DDD) sets are setting new standards, which may bring G & S into the classical fold without losing any of the original intentions. There are also some brand-new D'Oyly Carte sets, whose individually selected casts are listed. Truly excellent, they are also very expensive. Sullivan for the price of Beethoven! It may be wise to remember that in the less famous works, like *Patience*, for example, Gilbert's words are more important than Sullivan's music, which the latter knocked together at the last moment.

In the recording information which follows, (d) indicates that the recording includes dialogue.

The Gondoliers

Godfrey (d): **Decca 425 177-2 (2 CDs) $$ ADD**

Sargent: **EMI CMS7 54394-2 (2 CDs) $$ ADD**

Ross, Hanley, Fieldsend, Oke, Suart, D'Oyly Carte Opera, Pryce Jones (with *Di Ballo Overture*)
TER CDTER2 1187 (2 CDs) $$$ DDD

HMS Pinafore

Godfrey (d): **Decca 414 283-2 (2 CDs) $$ ADD**
Highlights: **Decca 436 145-2 $$ ADD**

Sargent: **EMI CMS7 64397-2 (2 CDs) $$ ADD**

R Evans, Palmer, Schade, Allen, Suart, Welsh National Opera, Mackerras
Telarc CD 80374 $$$ DDD (complete on one CD)

Ritchie, Roebuck, Gillett, Sandison, Grace, New Sadler's Wells O, Phipps
TER CDTER 1150 (2 CDs) $$$ DDD

Sullivan

Iolanthe

Godfrey (d): **Decca 414 145-2 (2 CDs) $$ ADD**

Sargent: **EMI CMS7 64400-2 (2 CDs) $$ ADD**

Hanley, Woollett, Pert, Blake Jones, Suart, D'Oyly Carte Opera, Pryce-Jones (with *Thespis* Suite)
TER CDTER2 1188 (2 CDs) $$$ DDD

See also *Mikado*

The Mikado

Masterson, Holland, Wright, Ayldon, D'Oyly Carte Opera, Nash
Decca 425 190-2 (2 CDs) $$ ADD
Highlights: **Decca 433 618-2 $$ ADD**

Sargent: **EMI CMS7 64403-2 (2 CDs) $$ ADD**

McLaughlin, Palmer, Rolfe Johnson, Suart, Adams, Welsh National Opera, Mackerras
Telarc CD 80284 $$$ DDD (complete on one CD)

Harwood, Begg, Moyle, Dowling, Shilling, Sadler's Wells Opera, Faris (with *Iolanthe* highlights)
Classics for Pleasure CDPD 4730 (2 CDs) $ ADD

Rees, Bottone, Roberts, Ducarel, D'Oyly Carte Opera, Pryce-Jones
TER CDTER2 1178 (2 CDs) $$$ DDD

Patience

Godfrey (d): **Decca 425 193-2 (2 CDs) $$ ADD**

Sargent (with *Irish Symphony*, Liverpool PO, Groves)
EMI CMS7 64406-2 (2 CDs) $$ ADD

The Pirates of Penzance

Godfrey (d): **Decca 425 196-2 (2 CDs) $$ ADD**
Highlights: **Decca 436 148-2 $$ ADD**

Sargent (with 4 overtures, Liverpool PO, Groves)
EMI CMS7 64409-2 (2 CDs) $$ ADD

R Evans, Knight, Ainsley, Suart, Van Allen, Welsh National Opera, Mackerras
Telarc CD 80353 $$$ DDD (complete on one CD)

Hill Smith, Creasy, Roberts, Gareth Jones, D'Oyly Carte Opera, Pryce-Jones
TER CDTER2 1177 (2 CDs) $$$ DDD

Ruddigore

Sargent (with *Merchant of Venice* and *The Tempest* incidental music, Birmingham SO, Dunn)
EMI CMS7 61142-2 (2 CDs) $$ ADD

Hill Smith, Sandison, J Davies, Ayldon, Sadler's Wells Opera, Phipps
TER CDTER2 1128 (2 CDs) $$$ ADD

The Yeomen of the Guard

McNair, Streit, Allen, Terfel, ASMF, Marriner (d)
Philips 438 138-2 (2 CDs) $$$ DDD

Sargent: **EMI CMS7 64415-2 (2 CDs) $$ ADD**

Harwood, Knight, Reed, Potter, Sandford, Adams, RPO, Sargent (with *Trial by Jury*, CGO, Godfrey)
Decca 417 358-2 (2 CDs) $$ ADD

Ross, Pert, Fieldsend, Gray, D'Oyly Carte Opera, Edwards
TER CDTER2 1195 (2 CDs) $$$ DDD

Tchaikovsky

TCHAIKOVSKY, Piotr (1840–1893)

Eugene Onegin ★ R d

Focile, Hvorostovsky, Shicoff, Anisimov, Orchestre de Paris, Bychkov
Philips 438 235-2 (2 CDs) $$$ DDD
Highlights: **Philips 442 384-2 $$$ DDD**

Kubiak, Weikl, Burrows, Ghiaurov, CGO, Solti
Decca 417 413-2 (2 CDs) $$$ ADD

Freni, Allen, Shicoff, Burchuladze, Dresden Staatskapelle, Levine
DG 423 959-2 (2 CDs) $$$ DDD
Highlights: **DG 445 467-2 $$ DDD**

(in English) Te Kanawa, Hampson, Rosenshein, F. Connell, Welsh National Opera, Mackerras
EMI CDS5 55004-2 (2 CDs) $$$ DDD

Lenski's Aria • *Act 2 (t)*
Tatiana's Letter Scene • *Act 1 (s)*
Gremin's Aria • *Act 3 (ba)*

Since the break-up of the Soviet Union, Russian operas and Russian singers have flooded Western opera houses and *Eugene Onegin* has been a major beneficiary. By far the best of Tchaikovsky's many stage works, it had a major bearing on his introspective character, because the Pushkin tale on which it is based reflected his own life at the time of composition; the homosexual composer entered a disastrous marriage to avoid a fate similar to that of his Onegin. The music is typical Tchaikovsky, hence easily assimilated, but the most famous pages are orchestral—the Waltz and the Polonaise. There have been many complete recordings, with few totally successful until recently; Russian discs were always inferior to ours and Western singers seldom caught the right inflection in this music.

    The Philips recording is probably the best, with the first of the post-Soviet emigrés, Dimitri Hvorostovsky, as a fine Onegin and the still young Italian Nuccia Focile surprisingly good as Tatiana. It is

Tchaikovsky

hard to ignore the Decca and DG versions, however. The non-Russian name stars seem to have learnt their lessons rather well. The recording in English is an ideal compromise. Well sung and recorded, it overcomes the difficulty of listening to as well as singing in a Slavonic language.

The Plot Tatiana falls in love with Onegin, who is not interested in marriage and callously creates a scene resulting in a duel with his friend Lenski, who is killed. Years later Tatiana is married to Prince Gremin when she meets Onegin again. His love is now rekindled, but she rejects him as he rejected her earlier.

THE TOP TEN
Basses in Operas
ON CD

Ferrucio FURLANETTO
Nicolai GHIAUROV
Kurt MOLL
Yevgeny NESTERENKO
Ruggero RAIMONDI
Samuel RAMEY
Karl RIDDERBUSCH
Matti SALMINEN
Cesare SIEPI
Martti TALVELA

Verdi

VERDI, Giuseppe (1813–1901)

Aida ★★★ R d

Caballé, Cossotto, Domingo, Cappuccilli, CGO, Muti
EMI CDS7 47271-2 (3 CDs) $$$ ADD
Highlights: **EMI CDM7 63450-2 $$ ADD**

Freni, Baltsa, Carreras, Cappuccilli, VPO, Karajan
EMI CMS7 69300-2 (3 CDs) $$ ADD

Tebaldi, Simionato, Bergonzi, MacNeil, VPO, Karajan
Decca 414 087-2 (3 CDs) $$ ADD
Highlights: **Decca 417 763-2 $$ ADD**

Milanov, Barbieri, Björling, Warren, Rome Opera, Perlea
BMG/RCA GD 86652-2 (mono) (3 CDs) $$ ADD
Highlights: **BMG/RCA GD 60201 $$ ADD**

Celeste Aida • Act 1 (t)
Triumphal March • Act 2 (ch)
Ritorna vincitor • Act 1 (s)
O patria mia • Act 3 (s)
La fatal pietra • Act 4 (t, s)

Everybody thinks of *Aida* as a grand spectacle. In reality, there is only the one short Triumphal Scene which demands the lot. You can set the rest of the score in pyramid-sized locations, yet *Aida* is only the eternal triangle of two women and one man, with Aida's father acting briefly as an interfering catalyst. On CD the spectacle is absent and the three voices and the way they are used are predominant. There are many more set pieces than those listed above, even though they are not heard as often in extract form.

All the greatest singers of recent years have made full recordings. Domingo has made no less than four with different partners, and two of the three digital CD sets feature his Radames; those with Millo (Sony S3K 45973) and Ricciarelli (DG 410 092-2) are nearly as good as the one I have listed. Carreras has a better supporting cast

Verdi

than Pavarotti (Decca 417 439-2). The older singers (Tebaldi, Björling etc.) are well worth considering and their sound quality leaves little to be desired.

| The Plot | Amneris, the daughter of the King of Egypt, wants the victorious warrior Radames as her husband, but he loves her slave Aida. Amonasro, Aida's father and king of the Ethiopians, who are about to attack again, is among the prisoners taken by Radames and tricks the lovers into betraying Egypt's battle plans. Radames is tried for treason and condemned to be buried alive. Aida joins him in his living tomb.

Un ballo in maschera (A Masked Ball) ★★ R d

M Price, Battle, Ludwig, Pavarotti, Bruson, National PO, Solti
Decca 410 210-2 (2 CDs) $$$ DDD
Highlights: **Decca 425 529-2 $$$ DDD**

L Price, Grist, Verrett, Bergonzi, Merrill, RCA Radio Italiana O, Leinsdorf
BMG/RCA GD 86645 (2 CDs) $$ ADD

Barstow, Jo, Quivar, Domingo, Nucci, VPO, Karajan
DG 427 635-2 (2 CDs) $$$ DDD
Highlights: **DG 429 415-2 $$$ DDD**

Eri tu • Act 3 (b)
Di tu se fedele • Act 1 (t)
Morrò, ma prima in grazia • Act 3 (s)
Ma se m'è forza pederti • Act 3 (t)
Saper vorreste • Act 3 (s)

For many years neglected, Verdi's *Masked Ball* has become a best-seller in recent years. And no wonder; it is full of delightful music and has a sound dramatic structure, however inaccurate it may be historically. Based on the assassination of Gustav III of Sweden during a masked ball in 1792, the connection exists solely in the final scene. The real man was a homosexual and his killing was political, not executed by a jealous husband. Productions today often use the Swedish names for the characters.

Verdi

There are many fine recordings and two of them are headed by sopranos named Price—the English Margaret is, if anything, even better than the more famous American Leontyne. And you could not want better tenors than the three represented here.

The Plot Riccardo is in love with Amelia, the wife of Renato. Both being fine and noble, the affair is not consummated, but conspirators plan to assassinate Riccardo and when Amelia's husband, his best friend Renato, witnesses a secret meeting of the lovers, he joins them and kills Riccardo during the masked ball of the title. The dying Riccardo reveals Amelia's innocence.

Don Carlos ★ R d

(in French) Ricciarelli, Valentini, Domingo, Nucci, Raimondi, Ghiaurov, La Scala Milan, Abbado
DG 415 316-2 (4 CDs) $$$ DDD
Highlights: **DG 415 981-2 $$$ DDD**

Caballé, Verrett, Domingo, Milnes, Raimondi, Foiani, CGO, Giulini
EMI CDS7 47701-8 (3 CDs) $$$ ADD
Highlights: **EMI CDM7 63089-2 $$ ADD**

Freni, Baltsa, Carreras, Cappuccilli, Ghiaurov, Raimondi, BPO, Karajan
EMI CMS7 69304-2 (3 CDs) $$ ADD

O don fatale • *Act 4 (ms)*
Ella giammai m'amò • *Act 4 (ba)*
Dio, che nell'alma infondere • *Act 2 (t, b)*
O Carlo, ascolta • *Act 4 (b)*

A genuine five-act French grand opera in the true sense of the word, *Don Carlos* is more famous in a later four-act Italian version, usually called *Don Carlo*. Apart from the names, none of the action is historically accurate; the real Carlos was a crippled homicidal maniac! The music is much weightier than other Verdi works, but very beautiful. The opera is too long, sprawling and gloomy for beginners to the opera field, but there are many famous set pieces and Verdi is never dull.

The only recording of the original is fine in every way, but does involve four CDs at full price. There is little to choose between the other two, but serious lovers of singing may like to consider the old mono EMI recording (CMS7 64642-2, 3 CDs, $$ ADD), which has two of the best performances ever recorded: Tito Gobbi's Rodrigo and Boris Christoff's Philip, not to mention Giulio Neri's Grand Inquisitor. Unfortunately, the tenor and soprano are not in the same class.

> [The Plot] Don Carlos, son of Philip II of Spain, is politically involved with the liberation of Flanders from Spanish rule and romantically involved with his father's young wife. The intervention of the Inquisition and a jealous woman (Eboli) cause both affairs to end disastrously. The ending leaves the fate of Don Carlos open to speculation.

Ernani ★★ R d

L Price, Bergonzi, Sereni, Flagello, RCA Italiana O, Schippers
BMG/RCA GD 86503 (2 CDs) $$ ADD

Freni, Domingo, Bruson, Ghiaurov, La Scala Milan, Muti
EMI CDS7 47083-2 (3 CDs) $$$ DDD

Ernani, involami • Act 1 (s)
O sommo Carlo • Act 3 (b, ch)
Infelice e tu credevi • Act 1 (ba)
Oh! de' verd'anni miei • Act (b)

The most ridiculous opera plot of them all, stuffed with the kind of rabble-rousing tunes which made Verdi a national hero. Anybody can start *Ernani* at any point and get a good tune. Only don't look at the story line; it doesn't bear inspection from the very beginning, which has Elvira in her bedroom facing a lover, a fiancé and a rapist all at the same time! But what music! The RCA set is a wonderful bargain, beautifully sung, the EMI a fine live performance, more costly, but digitally recorded.

> [The Plot] The revolutionary Ernani loves Elvira, who is the fiancée of Silva. Don Carlo, the King of Castile, tries to rape Elvira, but is stopped by Ernani. Enter Silva who, under the Spanish laws of chivalry, protects the 'guest' in his house (Ernani) and saves him from arrest. Ernani now owes his life to Silva and gives him a hunting horn: 'Blow the horn at any time and I will commit suicide'. Don Carlo is

Verdi

elected Charlemagne, Emperor of the Holy Roman Empire, forgives Elvira for not allowing herself to be raped, and gives her to Ernani. On their wedding night Silva blows the horn outside their window, and Ernani kills himself. (I did not invent this story; Victor Hugo did.)

Falstaff ★ R c

Bruson, Ricciarelli, Hendricks, Valentini, Nucci, Los Angeles PO, Giulini
DG 410 503-2 (2 CDs) $$$ DDD

Gobbi, Schwarzkopf, Merriman, Barbieri, Panerai, Philharmonia O, Karajan
EMI CDS7 49668-2 (2 CDs) $$$ ADD

Fischer-Dieskau, Ligabue, Resnik, Sciutti, Panerai, VPO, Bernstein
Sony M2K 42535 (2 CDs) $$ ADD

L'onore! ladri! • Act 1 (b)
E sogno? (Ford's monologue) • Act 2 (b)
Sul fil d'un soffio • Act 4 (s)

Verdi's *Falstaff* is unquestionably the greatest comic opera ever written, yet its subtlety is such that it needs an experienced opera lover to gather up its beauties. Here are none of the standard tunes which people have heard endlessly. Yet Verdi and his librettist Boito have come as close to musical Shakespeare as anybody ever has.

The three sets listed offer the best at three levels of time. The first is as up-to-date as they come—a later recording conducted by Solti is not in the running. Gobbi was always the great Falstaff and Karajan the expert conductor. Bernstein's brief stint at the Vienna State Opera was never better than in his *Falstaff* in the sixties and Fischer-Dieskau is more at home here than in other Italian parts.

The Plot The fat knight Falstaff fancies himself as a ladies' man. Mistresses Alice and Quickly trap him into an assignment in Windsor Forest, where the poor man is pummelled and humiliated by phoney fairies and goblins.

Verdi

La forza del destino (The Force of Destiny) ★★ R d

L Price, Domingo, Milnes, Giaiotti, LSO, Levine
BMG/RCA RD 81864 (3 CDs) $$$ ADD

Plowright, Carreras, Bruson, Burchuladze, Philharmonia O, Sinopoli
DG 419 203-2 (3 CDs) $$$ DDD
Highlights: **DG 423 148-2 $$$ DDD**

Arroyo, Bergonzi, Cappuccilli, Raimondi, RPO, Gardelli
EMI CDS7 64646-2 (3 CDs) $$ ADD

Highlights: Freni, Domingo, Zancanaro, Plishka, La Scala Milan, Muti
EMI CDS7 54326-2 $$$ DDD

Pace, pace • Act 4 (s)
Solenne in quest'ora • Act 3 (t, b)
La vergine degli angeli • Act 2 (s, ch)
Urna fatale • Act 3 (b)
Invano, Alvaro • Act 4 (t, b)

One of the best and the most flawed of the many Verdi operas; he never did stop tinkering with it and there are many ways of getting it right. The main point is that it is so full of magnificent set pieces which follow each other so rapidly that the whole does not add up to the sum of the parts. Nobody in this case wants to go back to the original, which was staged in St Petersburg of all places, but this music calls for great voices, and few opera houses can afford the kind of casts you get on CDs.

With so many major roles it is hard to find a perfect balance, the tenor once again being at the core of it all. I prefer Domingo and Bergonzi, in their different ways, to Carreras, but the latter's fans need have no fear.

The Plot Alvaro accidentally kills Leonora's father. Her brother, Carlo, starts a vendetta against him. Leonora becomes a hermit, while the two men fight again and again over many years in many locations. Alvaro takes holy vows, but is provoked into a final duel in which he mortally wounds Carlo, who kills Leonora before he dies.

Verdi

Macbeth ★ R d

Cossotto, Milnes, Carreras, Raimondi, New Philharmonia O, Muti
EMI CMS7 64339-2 (2 CDs) $$ ADD

Zampieri, Bruson, Shicoff, Lloyd, Deutsche Opera Berlin, Sinopoli
Philips 412 133-2 (3 CDs) $$$ DDD

Verrett, Cappuccilli, Domingo, La Scala Milan, Abbado
DG 415 688-2 (3 CDs) $$$ ADD
Highlights: **DG 435 414-2 $$ DDD**

Ah! la paterna mano • *Act 4 (t)*
Sleep-walking Scene • *Act 4 (s)*
La luce langue • *Act 2 (s)*

Strangely, the most famous aria from *Macbeth* constitutes almost the whole of the tenor part; Macduff has little else to sing. More strangely, Lady Macbeth, on two of the three recommended recordings, is sung by a mezzo-soprano, when her arias have been recorded by famous sopranos past and present. But Verdi asked for the voice of a 'she-devil'. While the opera itself belongs to Verdi's 'galley years', when he was still concentrating on good tunes, it shows the way to the gloominess of later works and is not for beginners.

In this case the unlisted older sets are no match for more recent ones. The EMI of 1976 is by far the best buy on two instead of three CDs at mid-price and (a minor point?) is also the best sung! Verrett/Cappuccilli are close behind, but on three full-priced discs and not even digitally recorded. The conducting and DDD recording of the Sinopoli make it worthy of inclusion.

The Plot Macbeth and his wife kill the king of Scotland and usurp the throne. Remorse sends Lady Macbeth to madness and death, while Macbeth himself is defeated in battle by the rightful heir.

Verdi

Nabucco ★★ R d

Suliotis, Gobbi, Prevedi, Cava, Vienna Opera, Gardelli
Decca 417 407-2 (2 CDs) $$$ ADD
Highlights: **Decca 421 867-2 $$ ADD**

Dimitrova, Cappuccilli, Domingo, Nesterenko, Deutsche Opera Berlin, Sinopoli
DG 410 512-2 (2 CDs) $$$ DDD
Highlights: **DG 439 493-2 $$ DDD**

Va pensiero • *Act 3 (ch)*
Tu sul labbro • *Act 2 (ba)*

The sensational Decca recording helped to somersault this first of Verdi's early successes into universal acceptance. Rarely heard before the fifties and, apart from the famous chorus of Hebrew prisoners, without any famous arias, *Nabucco* has an urgency of dramatic appeal which sets the music alight. There is no light relief, but the sad parts are gloriously tuneful and the action scenes so brilliant that you cannot but be convinced.

As in *Macbeth*°, the tenor has only a small part; the soprano and baritone share the glory, with the bass featured in two major arias. The above two sets are vastly better than any other recording. Vocally, the Decca is unlikely ever to be bettered. Suliotis recorded the part at the age of twenty-two and ruined her voice forever. But her Abigaille can only be described as superlative. And Gobbi is at his very best as Nabucco. Dimitrova and Cappuccilli have digital sound and are very good indeed.

| The Plot | Nabucco, King of Babylon, proclaims himself God and is struck by lightning, which leaves him mad. His illegitimate daughter Abigaille takes over as ruler from the rightful heir, Fenana. Nabucco regains his sanity and accepts Jehovah as the nation's only god. Abigaille commits suicide.

Verdi

Otello ★★ R d

Studer, Domingo, Leiferkus, Bastille Opera, Chung
DG 439 805-2 (2 CDs) $$$ DDD
Highlights: **DG 445 867-2 $$$ DDD**

Rysanek, Vickers, Gobbi, Rome Opera, Serafin
BMG/RCA GD 81969 (2 CDs) $$ ADD

Te Kanawa, Pavarotti, Nucci, Chicago SO, Solti
Decca 433 669-2 (2 CDs) $$$ DDD
Highlights: **Decca 440 843-2 $$$ DDD**

Highlights: Ricciarelli, Domingo, Díaz, La Scala Milan, Maazel
EMI 7 89059 2-555 $$$ DDD

Credo in un Dio crudel (Iago's Creed) • Act 2 (b)
Salce, salce (Willow Song) • Act 4 (s)
Si pel ciel • Act 2 (t, b)
Dio, mi potevi scagliar • Act 3 (t)

All round, *Otello* is probably the best amalgamation of sound and word ever produced by any composer. This is truly great music without a moment's waste in sound or words, condensing Shakespeare's play most faithfully and using his actual text (in Italian) throughout. Most of the great moments have been recorded on their own, yet no aria except Iago's 'Credo' has ever become universally popular. This should stop no one from acquiring this wonderful work.

Domingo has dominated the part for years and his most recent (third) recording is the best in every way. The best Iago of all is Tito Gobbi, whose Otello, John Vickers, is poignantly sung and acted. Pavarotti's recording was made during a concert series; he has never sung it on stage and never will. His voice lacks both the baritonal timbre favoured today and the heroic ring of Del Monaco, or Tamagno, who created the part. Studer, Te Kanawa and Rysanek, in that order, are all first class as Desdemona.

The Plot Iago, for political reasons, destroys Otello by making it appear that his wife is unfaithful. The possessively jealous Otello kills her and then himself, while Iago's wiles are exposed by his own wife.

Verdi

Rigoletto ★★★ R d

Gruberová, Shicoff, Bruson, Fassbaender, St Cecilia Rome O, Sinopoli
Philips 412 592-2 (2 CDs) $$$ DDD
Highlights: **Philips 432 629-2 $$ DDD**

Sutherland, Pavarotti, Milnes, Tourangeau, LSO, Bonynge
Decca 414 269-2 (2 CDs) $$$ ADD
Highlights: **Decca 421 303-2 $$ ADD**

Callas, Di Stefano, Gobbi, Lazzarini, La Scala Milan, Serafin
EMI CDS7 47469-8 (mono) (2 CDs) $$$ ADD

La donna è mobile • *Act 4 (t)*
Caro Nome • *Act 2 (s)*
Bella figlia dell'amore (Quartet) • *Act 4 (t, s, b, ms)*
Questa o quella • *Act 1 (t)*
Cortigiani, vil razza • *Act 3 (b)*

Verdi's most popular opera, which contains his most universally famous arias. It also marked the turning point in Verdi's career, moving from set pieces to continuous music. No opera collection can be without it and there have been numerous recordings over the years. I have chosen the two best current sets and the classic mono recording by the most famous singing trio of the century, Maria Callas, Giuseppe di Stefano and Tito Gobbi. The top choice contains the least familiar names, but the three principals sing with real distinction. The names in the Decca set speak for themselves.

| The Plot | Gilda, daughter of Rigoletto, the court jester, is seduced by the Duke of Mantua. Rigoletto hires a hitman to kill the Duke, but Gilda, stupid girl, loves him so much that she takes his place and is killed instead.

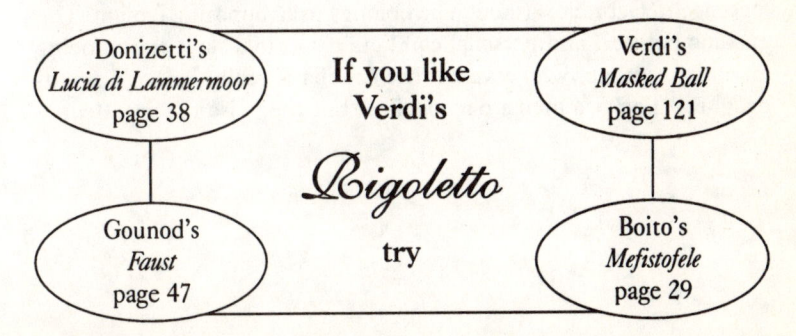

If you like Verdi's *Rigoletto* **try**

- Donizetti's *Lucia di Lammermoor* page 38
- Verdi's *Masked Ball* page 121
- Gounod's *Faust* page 47
- Boito's *Mefistofele* page 29

Verdi

Simon Boccanegra ★ R d

Freni, Carreras, Cappuccilli, Ghiaurov, La Scala Milan, Abbado
DG 415 692-2 (2 CDs) $$$ ADD

Te Kanawa, Aragall, Nucci, Burchuladze, La Scala Milan, Solti
Decca 425 628-2 (2 CDs) $$$ DDD

De los Angeles, Campora, Gobbi, Christoff, Rome Opera, Santini
EMI CMS7 63513-2 (mono) (2 CDs) $$ ADD

Il lacerato spirito • *Prologue (ba)*
Plebe! Patrizi • *Act 1 (b, s, t, ch)*
Figlia! a tal nome • *Act 1 (b, s)*

Another of the 'doctored' Verdi operas, a work whose main attraction, the Council Chamber Scene, was added twenty-three years after its first performance! There is some beautiful music in *Simon Boccanegra*, but it is rather drawn out and peters out somewhat lamely. The opportunities for great singing are there, however.

Once more, here is a Verdi opera with the baritone, not the tenor, in the centre, though tenor, soprano and bass get ample opportunities. For once, there is a part ideally suited to Carreras, and Cappuccilli is better as Simone than he was in an earlier set with Domingo and Ricciarelli (BMG/RCA RD 70729, 2 CDs, $$$ ADD). Te Kanawa is the glory of the other set, but the mono recording has not only Victoria de los Angeles in great form, but Tito Gobbi and Boris Christoff duplicating their successful partnership in *Don Carlos*°.

> [The Plot] The Doge of Venice (Simone Boccanegra) is opposed by Fiesco, who has, without his knowledge, brought up Simone's daughter, Amelia. The girl is reunited with her father, who agrees to her marriage to Gabriele, although he belongs to an opposing faction. The ensuing political and personal conflicts result in a slow poison being taken by Simone, who reveals that Amelia is really Fiesco's granddaughter. The two men are reconciled, but the poison takes effect.

Verdi

La traviata ★★★ R d

Sutherland, Pavarotti, Manuguèrra, National PO, Bonynge
Decca 430 491-2 (2 CDs) $$$ ADD
Highlights: **Decca 400 057-2 $$$ DDD**

Gruberová, Shicoff, Zancanaro, LSO, Rizzi
Teldec 9031-76348-2 (2 CDs) $$$ DDD
Highlights: **Teldec 4509-91975-2 $$$ DDD**

Cotrubas, Domingo, Milnes, OC, Kleiber
DG 415 132-2 (2 CDs) $$$ ADD
Highlights: **DG 435 417-2 $$$ ADD**

Libiamo! (Drinking Song) • Act 1 (t, s, ch)
É strano ... sempre libera • Act 1 (s)
De' miei bollenti spiriti • Act 2 (t)
Di provenza il mar • Act 2 (b)
Addio del passato • Act 3 (s)
Parigi, o cara • Act 3 (t, s)

The best weepie in the repertoire, *Traviata* has a wealth of famous melodies which run throughout without interruption. The vehicle for all the greatest sopranos over the years, there have been endless complete recordings and the number of CD sets makes it hard indeed to make an authoritative choice.

Several recent recordings have had the kind of mixed 'very good' and 'very bad' reviews, making serious recommendation quite

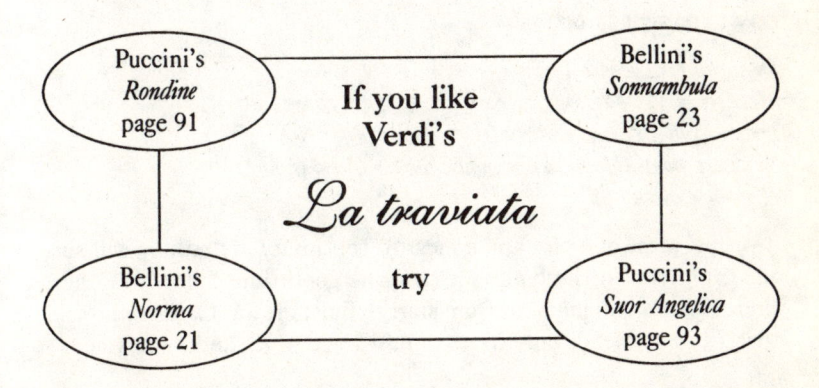

If you like Verdi's *La traviata* try

- Puccini's *Rondine* page 91
- Bellini's *Sonnambula* page 23
- Bellini's *Norma* page 21
- Puccini's *Suor Angelica* page 93

difficult. Sutherland has recorded it twice and Callas thrice, but two of the latter's are live performances issued many years after her death. (The 1958 Lisbon is best, with Kraus as an excellent Alfredo, but the sound is poor; EMI CDS7 49187-2, mono, 2 CDs, $$$ ADD.) Gruberová unexpectedly turns up trumps in the last act in the only digital recommended recording, but her Alfredo is not as good as Domingo with Cotrubas.

The Plot The consumptive courtesan Violetta falls in love with Alfredo, but is talked out of living with him by his father; the family's honour is more important. Violetta leaves Alfredo. By the time the father realises that hers is a true love, it is too late. She dies in Alfredo's arms.

Il trovatore ★★★ R d

Millo, Zajick, Domingo, Chernov, Morris, Metropolitan Opera, Levine
Sony S2K 48070 (2 CDs) $$$ DDD

L Price, Cossotto, Domingo, Milnes, Giaiotto, New Philharmonia O, Mehta
BMG/RCA RD 86194 (2 CDs) $$$ ADD

Milanov, Barbieri, Björling, Warren, Moscona, RCA Victor O, Cellini
BMG/RCA GD 86643 (mono) (2 CDs) $$ ADD
Highlights: **BMG/RCA GD 60191-2 (mono) $$ ADD**

Highlights: Plowright, Fassbaender, Domingo, Zancanaro, St Cecilia Rome O, Giulini
DG 415 285-2 $$$ DDD

Di quella pira • Act 3 (t)
Miserere • Act 4 (t, s)
D'amor sull'ali rosee • Act 4 (s)
Ai nostri monti (Home to our mountains) • Act 4 (t, ms)
Il balen • Act 2 (b)

A mess of a plot and a mess of continuity, *Il trovatore* will survive on the bare fact that one good tune follows another; there is not a dull moment from start to finish. It was Caruso who said that *Trovatore* needs only three things: voice, voice and more voice.

It is hard indeed to find ideal matchings in all five voice categories, but the sky is the limit with record companies since exclusive recording contracts are no longer being signed by the best artists; Domingo has recorded the opera for RCA, Deutsche Grammophon and, in 1994, Sony. His Leonora, Aprile Millo, is superb and the Russian Vladimir Chernov is one of the best De Lunas of all time. Both the earlier Domingo sets are the next choices, but I have included the cheaper historic Milanov/Björling in place of the pretty good Callas/Di Stefano without Gobbi (EMI CDS7 49347-2, 2 CDs, $$$ ADD). Strangely, the Sutherland/ Pavarotti set (Decca 417-137-2, 3 CDs, $$$ ADD) is not only the least good, but by far the most expensive.

| The Plot | Leonora is loved by both Manrico and the Count de Luna, who are at war with each other. Manrico tries to save his supposed mother, Azucena, but is captured by De Luna. Leonora offers herself to him in exchange for Manrico's life, but takes a slow-acting poison. In ignorance of the latter fact, Manrico is furious at her infidelity. She dies before his eyes and he is executed as Azucena tells De Luna that he has killed his own brother.

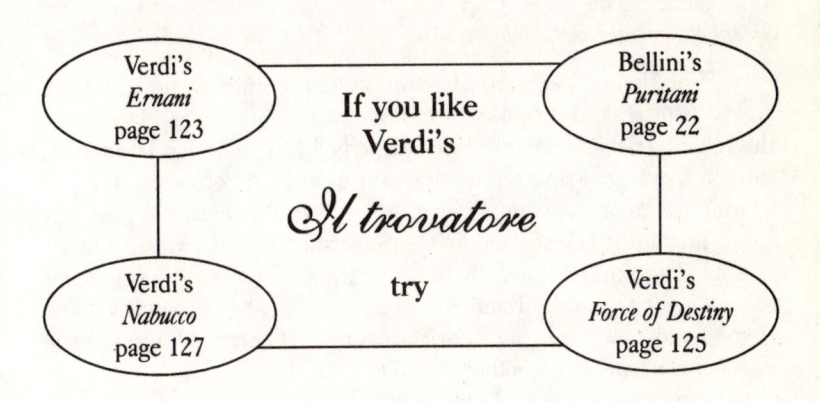

If you like Verdi's *Il trovatore* try:

- Verdi's *Ernani* page 123
- Bellini's *Puritani* page 22
- Verdi's *Nabucco* page 127
- Verdi's *Force of Destiny* page 125

WAGNER, Richard (1813–1883)

Der fliegende Holländer (The Flying Dutchman) ★ R d

Behrends, Hale, Rydl, Protschka, VPO, Dohnányi
Decca 436 418-2 (2 CDs) $$$ DDD

Balslev, Estes, Salminen, Schunk, Bayreuth Festival, Nelsson
Philips 434 599-2 (2 CDs) $$ DDD
Highlights: **Philips 434 221 $$ DDD**

Vejzovic, Van Dam, Moll, Hofmann, BPO, Karajan
EMI CMS7 64650-2 (2 CDs) $$ DDD
Highlights: **EMI 7 63449-2 555 $$$ DDD**

Jo-ho-hoe (Senta's Ballad) • Act 2 (s)
Die Frist ist um • Act 1 (b)
Mit Gewitter und Sturm • Act 1 (t)
Steuermann, lass die Wacht • Act 3 (t)
Spinning Chorus • Act 2 (ch)

The first of the operas written by the mature Wagner, and the shortest, the *Dutchman* has one of his more sensible stories, though mysticism already rears its ugly head. Not for beginners, though there are some stunning choruses and one or two tunes still bearing traces of the young Wagner's 'bel canto' operas.

The latest (Decca) is the best recording in every way. All other sets have weaknesses, usually in the casting of Senta; Vejzovic is not bad, but not as good as Karajan's other singers. The Bayreuth version is good and completely authentic, of course. There is an ultra-cheap excellent Naxos set (8.660025, 2 CDs, $ DDD).

The Plot The Dutchman is cursed to sail the seven seas forever, unless he can find a woman who will be faithful unto death. Those who love him and fail are eternally damned. He renounces Senta to save her from this fate and sails away. She promptly jumps into the sea and they both find salvation.

Wagner

Lohengrin ★★ R d

Norman, Randová, Domingo, Nimsgern, Sotin, VPO, Solti
Decca 421 053-2 (4 CDs) $$$ DDD
Highlights: **Decca 425 530-2 $$$ DDD**

Studer, Meier, Jerusalem, Welker, Moll, VPO, Abbado
DG 437 808-2 (3 CDs) $$$ DDD
Highlights: **DG 445 869-2 $$$ DDD**

Grümmer, Ludwig, J Thomas, Fischer-Dieskau, Frick, VPO, Kempe
EMI CDS7 49017-2 (3 CDs) $$$ ADD
Highlights: **EMI 7 49017-2-667 $$$ ADD**

In fernem Land (Lohengrin's Narration) • *Act 3 (t)*
Einsam in trüben Tagen (Elsa's Dream) • *Act 1 (s)*
Wedding March • *Act 3 (ch)*
Das süsse Lied verhallt (Love Duet) • *Act 3 (t, s)*

Probably the most accessible of all the Wagner operas, though, as always with him, far too long for beginners. His mythology also is at fault. If Lohengrin was the son of Parsifal, how could Parsifal be untouched by woman? Eschenbach's original story *Parzifal* offers an explanation; Wagner does not.

The Decca Solti recording takes four instead of three CDs, but it does have a fine combination in Domingo, the best Lohengrin surely, and Jessye Norman. Abbado's Ortrud is the best of them all and Rudolf Kempe's fine conducting and excellent cast are holding their own thirty years after issue; the American Jess Thomas was the best Lohengrin of the sixties! Who would have expected a Spaniard (Domingo) to take his crown?

The Plot Elsa is accused of killing her brother. Lohengrin becomes her champion and husband on condition that she never ask his name and origin. The evil Telramund and his wife Ortrud sow seeds of doubt in Elsa's mind and she demands Lohengrin's secret on their wedding night. The question is answered in public. End of marriage.

Wagner

Die Meistersinger von Nürnberg
(The Mastersingers of Nuremberg) ★ R c

Studer, Heppner, Weikl, Moll, Bavarian State O, Sawallisch
EMI CDS5 55142 (4 CDs) $$$ DDD

Ligendza, Domingo, Fischer-Dieskau, Lagger, Deutsche Oper Berlin, Jochum
DG 415 278-2 (4 CDs) $$$ ADD
Highlights: **DG 445 470-2 $$$ ADD**

Schwarzkopf, Hopf, Edelmann, Dalberg, Bayreuth Festival, Karajan
EMI CMS7 64154-2 (mono) (4 CDs) $$ ADD

Highlights: Donath, Kollo, Adam, Ridderbusch, Dresden Staatskapelle, Karajan
EMI CDM7 63455-2 $$ ADD

Morgenlich leuchtend (Prize Song) • Act 3 (t)
Fliedermonolog • Act 2 (b)
Am stillen Herd • Act 1 (t)
Selig, wie die Sonne • Act 3 (s, t, b, t, ms)

Die Meistersinger is surely the longest comedy ever written but, because of its touching sentimentality, it seldom produces any laughter. The whole thing is just too true to life, be it in the fifteenth century, when the real Hans Sachs was alive, the nineteenth, when Wagner wrote the opera, or the twentieth, when it was recorded frequently and seldom successfully.

There was no new recording for nearly twenty years before the recent Sawallisch recording was made, and that is not outstanding either. It is probably as good as any produced to date and digital sound is certainly an asset for anything as huge as this work. Ben Heppner at the moment looks like a major tenor star in the making and Studer is already the most important, and the most versatile, soprano around. But Jochum had Fischer-Dieskau and Domingo, and the 1950 mono Karajan set has a cast unlikely to be bettered. Even the normally dry Hans Hopf began to shine in this live performance, while the young Schwarzkopf was in glorious voice.

The Plot The knight Walther von Stolzing seeks to enter the Guild of Mastersingers in Nuremberg to win the hand of Eva. He is frustrated by Beckmesser, a suitor for Eva's hand, who insists on sticking to the rules, which Walther's new poetry breaks. Their wise leader, Hans Sachs, helps Walther to win both the song contest and Eva.

Der Ring des Nibelungen   R d

*N*obody who buys this book is likely to need a complete *Ring* cycle of roughly fourteen CDs—roughly, because conductors have been known to have differences of nearly two hours in the total length of the four works! Wagner's monumental work is big news and people pay big money to see complete cycles, preferably in Bayreuth. Dare I say that the majority do so for the sake of boasting of having sat through it? All credit to Wagner fans, but he is an acquired taste and, apart from *Die Walküre°*, which lasts nearly four hours, not counting intervals, none of the other three operas holds much interest for the novice.

Tannhäuser   ★ R d

(Paris version) Studer, Baltsa, Domingo, Schmidt, Philharmonia O, Sinopoli
DG 427 625-2 (3 CDs) $$$ DDD
Highlights: **DG 429 789-2 $$ DDD**

(Paris version) Dernesch, Ludwig, Kollo, Braun, VPO, Solti
Decca 414 581-2 (3 CDs) $$$ ADD

(Dresden version) Silja, Bumbry, Windgassen, Waechter, Bayreuth Festival, Sawallisch
Philips 434 607-2 (3 CDs) $$ ADD

O du mein holder Abendstern (O Star of Eve) • *Act 3 (b)*
Dich, teure Halle (Elisabeth's Greeting) • *Act 2 (s)*
Allmächt'ge Jungfrau (Elisabeth's Prayer) • *Act 3 (s)*
Pilgrim's Chorus • *Act 3 (ch)*

*N*ext to *Lohengrin°*, this is the most popular Wagner opera, with plenty of spectacle, fine choruses and, we hope, good singers. The title role is exceptionally difficult to sing and Tannhäuser has no popular aria; the extended 'Rome Narration' is a bloody bore when badly sung. One consequence: few recordings.

Wagner

There are two versions: the Paris one adds the long *Venusberg* scene to provide the compulsory ballet; the Dresden version is a classic live Bayreuth performance with the best singers of the sixties and some audience noise. Of the two 'Paris' tenors, Domingo still astounds and René Kollo is not as reliable, but at times has the edge on him. The ladies in the Solti are a little better than Studer and Baltsa, but there is little to choose between the sets. The digitality of the Sinopoli set is unimportant, the Solti sound is so good.

The Plot After dwelling in the arms of Venus, Tannhäuser returns to the land of the living to take part in a song competition. He blasphemes in his poetic outpourings and has to make the long trek to Rome to atone for his sins. The pope refuses to absolve him, but his lady-friend Elisabeth prays for him and dies. That saves his bacon.

Tristan und Isolde ★ R d

Nilsson, Ludwig, Windgassen, Talvela, Waechter, Bayreuth Festival, Böhm
DG 419 889-2 (3 CDs) $$$ ADD
Highlights: **DG 439 469-2 $$$ ADD**

Dernesch, Ludwig, Vickers, Ridderbusch, Berry, BPO, Karajan
EMI CMS7 69319-2 (4 CDs) $$ ADD

Flagstad, Thebom, Suthaus, Greindl, Fischer-Dieskau, Philharmonia O, Furtwängler
EMI CDS7 47322-8 (mono) (4 CDs) $$$ ADD

Mild und leise (Liebestod) • Act 3 (s)
O sink' hernieder (Love Duet) • Act 2 (t, s)

The legendary love story which is quoted in several operas written before Wagner ever thought of the subject. The 'Prelude and Liebestod', with or without the soprano, is a standard concert item, also often recorded on its own. *Tristan* is a simple tale which takes an awfully long time to tell. However lyrically beautiful, the poor tenor's death throes last twenty minutes; the soprano manages it in fifteen without even the help of poison or dagger; she dies of love—the 'Liebestod'.

With a new Barenboim *Tristan* starring current best singers (Jerusalem/Meier/Salminen; Teldec 4509945682, 4 CDs, $$$ DDD) not yet to hand, it is difficult to be unequivocal, but the older sets will probably hold up well. Böhm and Karajan run side by side, even price-wise. One is three CDs at full price, the other four at medium, Nilsson slightly better than Dernesch and Vickers superior to Windgassen, whose performance is live. And then there is Flagstad and Furtwängler, surely a historical pair if ever there was one. What does it matter that Schwarzkopf sang the top Cs in the 'Love Duet' for the aging Flagstad?

The Plot Tristan fetches Isolde as a bride for King Marke. Isolde commands a poisoned cup for herself and Tristan, but Brangäne substitutes a love potion. When they become lovers they are discovered and Tristan allows himself to be mortally wounded. After his death Isolde kicks the bucket.

Die Walküre (The Valkyrie) ★ R d

Nilsson, Rysanek, King, Adam, Bayreuth Festival, Böhm
Philips 412 478-2 (4 CDs) $$$ ADD

Nilsson, Crespin, King, Hotter, VPO, Solti
Decca 414 105-2 (4 CDs) $$$ ADD
Highlights: **Decca 421 887-2 $$ ADD**

Marton, Studer, Goldberg, Morris, Bavarian Radio SO, Haitink
EMI CDS7 49534-2 (4 CDs) $$$ DDD
Highlights: **EMI CDC7 54328-2 $$$ DDD**

The Ride of the Valkyries • Act 3 (ch)
Winterstürme wichen • Act 1 (t)
Du bist der Lenz • Act 1 (s)
Wotan's Farewell • Act 3 (ba)

The first of the three operas which make up *The Ring of the Nibelung*°; the fourth (*Das Rheingold*) is described as a 'preliminary evening' and is a kind of background briefing for the other three works. *Die Walküre* alone among the *Ring* operas has any musical extracts which are universally known. The 'Ride of the Valkyries' is almost corny in its constant reappearances, genuinely used (as in the film *Apocalypse Now*) or comically (as in Bugs Bunny cartoons). There are some great singing opportunities, if the voices are big enough, but four hours plus is more than enough for most people; highlights are more appropriate.

Wagner

There have been many recordings of the work over the years, but never a totally satisfactory one. In Wagner the conductor often plays a larger part than the singers, but the best conductor needs a well-balanced cast. Duplications of famous singers in recordings occur regularly; for example, James Morris recorded Wotan for two competing companies in the same year, there being no better around. Thus, two of the three recommended sets have the same Brünnhilde and Siegmund, but different conductors, and both came from the sixties. There are two digital recordings, neither as good as the older ones. The alternative to Haitink on EMI is DG's Levine with an all-star Metropolitan Opera cast (Behrends, Norman, Lakes, Morris, Moll, DG 423 389-2, 4 CDs, $$$ DDD) which somehow does not jell.

The Plot The hunted Siegmund seeks shelter in the home of Hunding and his wife Sieglinde. The latter is Siegmund's sister, but they fall in love anyway. Wotan, the ruler of Valhalla, is determined that Siegmund must die in his battle with Hunding, but Wotan's daughter, Brünnhilde, tries to protect him, unsuccessfully. As punishment Wotan sends her into a magic sleep. Sieglinde survives carrying Siegmund's child, which will grow up to become Siegfried in the next opera of the cycle.

WEBER, Carl Maria von (1786–1826)

Der Freischütz ★ R d

Grümmer, Otto, Schock, Prey, Kohn, BPO, Keilberth
EMI CMS7 69342-2 (2 CDs) $$ ADD

Janowitz, Mathis, Schreier, Weikl, Adam, Dresden Staatskapelle, Kleiber
DG 415 432-2 (2 CDs) $$$ ADD
Highlights: **DG 439 440-2 $$$ ADD**

Sweet, Ziesak, Seiffert, Schmidt, Rydl, Berlin SO, Janowski
BMG/RCA 09026 62538-2 (2 CDs) $$$ DDD

Leise, leise • Act 2 (s)
Durch die Wälder, durch die Auen • Act 1 (t)
Und ob die Wolke • Act 3 (s)

The opera which started the romantic movement in 1821. Still as effective as ever, here you will find the association of horn calls and forests, of magic and mystery instead of intrigues and murder. The music is surprisingly light, except for the casting of spells in the Wolf's Glen. But its unfamiliar German folk idiom makes it less readily accessible than Italian operas of its kind.

Freischütz has been fortunate in its recordings; there are many more than the listed good ones. The oldest of them all (EMI) is in many ways still the best, but the latest (1994) features Sharon Sweet, whose voice is very much what her name implies, and it has digital sound, which is important in the scenes of magic-making.

The Plot The huntsman Max needs to win a shooting tournament to win Agathe. He makes a pact to produce seven magic bullets, the first six of which are bound to hit their mark, while the seventh will find a target chosen by Samiel, Weber's Mephisto. The bullet kills the villain who has tempted Max, instead of the planned Agathe.

GREAT *Singers* OF THE PAST

Many hundreds of CD recitals of historical singers have been released on CD and new ones appear every month. Recording copyrights expire after fifty years and anybody can (and does) re-issue any of the older recordings, including many complete opera sets. These are for the specialist collector, not the reader of this book.

I cannot, however, ignore the fact that it has often been written, and written truly: 'Caruso made the gramophone; the gramophone did not make Caruso'. Recording techniques in the early years favoured the male voice. Caruso was the world's most famous singer and, consequently, people all over the world bought the primitive wind-up gramophones to hear the man whose live audiences were limited when the wireless had not yet been invented. At the turn of the century it was far from certain that recording sound (or making films) had any useful future. Caruso was the man who proved otherwise.

Caruso joined the Australian Nellie Melba late in her career. While her fame was as great as his, she was declining as recording techniques improved, while Caruso's fame increased throughout his life; he died at the age of 48 in the very prime of his life. Neither ever recorded a complete, or even incomplete, opera, but their records may be of interest to readers. Note that composers are listed only for those operas which do not appear in the main text.

CARUSO, Enrico, *tenor* (1873–1921, Italy)

By far the most famous singer of all time, and likely to remain so. Why this man's voice (on primitive recordings) has appealed to so many generations is a mystery, for nobody has ever

Caruso

claimed that Caruso was perfect; nor was he. Yet his voice continues to hold universal appeal and seventy-five years after he made his last records they still sell in thousands on the most modern recording system, the CD. You can buy every record ever made by Caruso on a twelve-CD set (RCA GD 60495), and that set has been a best-seller world-wide! Furthermore, a huge number of Caruso CDs are bought *and played* by the general public in spite of the, by modern standards, inferior sound quality.

Caruso's is the only voice of the so-called 'Golden Age of Singing' which can give pleasure to the modern ear in the same way as any brand new recording. Melba may be equally famous, particularly in Australia, but the average person would not buy a Melba CD to play for the sheer enjoyment of listening to it. No wonder every Tom, Dick and Harriet, who would not know the difference between Puccini and Mozart, knows who Caruso was and, on disc, still is. His voice continues to be not just admired, but enjoyed.

There is a huge number of Caruso CDs on the market and, unfortunately, sound engineers have spent years in trying to recapture the 'real Caruso' by technical means. Ignore all claims that this or that system is closer to the original. Dozens of Caruso CDs exist which are sonically and sometimes even vocally a travesty of the real thing. Reproductions made from the original masters are for the serious collector, not the average person. Because of their immense sales originally, what you hear on them is the tail end of a long production line, full of surface noise, clicks and distortions which do not exist on dubbings taken from mint copies in private collections.

A Caruso disc bought to be enjoyed like any other should come from the stable of companies like Nimbus or Pearl or the occasional 'commercial' CD produced by the original manufacturers. Always remember that Caruso belonged to a long-lost generation of singers whose standards were different from ours, but the voice itself has something which no other tenor has ever had or will have. It is not just unique, but unique in that it has lost none of its appeal after all these years.

'Caruso': *Elisir d'amore, Pagliacci, Manon, Aida, Rigoletto, Trovatore, Juive, Tosca, Manon Lescaut, Ballo in maschera, Forza del destino, Africana* (Meyerbeer), *Duca d'Alba* (Donizetti), *Regina di Saba* (Goldmark), *Don Sebastiano* (Donizetti), *Lo Schiavo* (Gomes)
Nimbus NI 7803

'Caruso 1': *Rigoletto, Aida, Forza del destino, Ballo in maschera, Tosca* (2), *Pagliacci* (2), *Otello* (2) (with Ruffo), *Africana* (Meyerbeer), *Bohème* (Puccini) (3) (with Melba & Scotti), *Bohème* (Leoncavallo), *Trovatore* (3) (with Schumann-Heink), O sole mio, A vucchella, Parted
Pearl GEMMCD 9309

MELBA, Nellie, *soprano* (1861–1931, Australia)

Nobody doubts that Melba was the most famous soprano of her time and many of her recordings prove this beyond doubt, even though she did not begin to record before the age of forty-three. It is an unfortunate fact that the early gramophone took more kindly to male voices than high sopranos, with the result that listening to a recording of Melba is not as pleasurable as listening to a Caruso CD. It is necessary to adjust one's enjoyment level for Melba discs, which, like Caruso's, can come from unauthorised primitive copies or reputable (and more expensive) quality firms. Sitting down and listening to a continuous row of Melba recordings is not recommended. The lady was a great singer and she does do some wonderful things, but an all-Melba CD recital is simply too long for continuous enjoyment. And, unlike Caruso's, too many CDs of Melba's recordings are decidedly inferior in quality.

It should also be remembered that the Melba legend, propagated by herself, is largely fictitious. It is no reflection on her magnificent singing to point out that it was not she who made 'Home, Sweet Home' popular—she was only following in the voice-steps of her even more famous predecessor, Adelina Patti; that her dameship was given for fundraising, not singing; and that young singers should ignore anyone who teaches the 'Marchesi method' because Melba claimed she used it—she did not. Perhaps the lady was not a tramp, but she was neither truthful nor musically educated. She was a singer in an age when the singer was king (queen) and that was all that mattered. And that is all that we need to know today.

'Nellie Melba': *Rigoletto, Traviata, Bohème, Faust, Hamlet, Otello, Louise, Re Pastore* (Mozart), *Roi d'Ys* (Lalo), *Don César de Bazan* (Massenet) & songs by Arditi, Hahn, Debussy, Bemberg, Dvořák & folk songs
RCA 09026 61412-2

Melba

'Dame Nellie Melba 1': *Lucia di Lammermoor, Hamlet* (2), *Rigoletto* (with McCormack, etc.), *Traviata* (with Brownlee), *Tosca, Otello* (2), *Bohème, Lohengrin, Marriage of Figaro, Roi d'Ys* (Lalo), *L'allegro, il penseroso* (Handel), Pur dicesti, Comin' through the rye, Annie Laurie, Wings of a Dove, Farewell Speech, etc.
Pearl GEMMCD 9353

24 GREAT *Singers*
ON CD OPERA SETS

In this section are my assessments of some of the most famous singers who appear on complete opera recordings on CD in this book. I have omitted the few historical singers (like Gigli, Caniglia or Albanese) whose complete 78 rpm sets are available on CD—their place in the history of recordings is secure. The purpose of this guide is to help the newcomer to opera to get the most satisfaction from the new medium in sound as well as vocal values. Note that composers are listed only for those operas which do not appear in the main text.

BARTOLI, Cecilia, *mezzo-soprano* (b. 1966, Italy)

By far the biggest name in the mezzo-soprano field today, Bartoli certainly deserves all the praise she gets and to date she has not yet made a record which has not been first-class. She obviously has brains as well as a voice, because she husbands her instrument carefully by not appearing in big opera houses or in parts which are too heavy for her. The voice as such is a small one, which may grow in time, but she will never be another Marilyn Horne. Bartoli was launched with an enormous fanfare by her record company, Decca, and certainly produced the expected results. Her speciality is Rossini, with Mozart close behind. Her discs are unlikely to be superseded in the foreseeable future.

'Rossini Arias': *Cenerentola, Tancredi, Otello, Stabat Mater, Donna del lago, Pietra del paragone, Italiana in Algeri* (2)
Decca 425 430-2

'Mozart Portraits': *Così fan tutte* (3); *Marriage of Figaro* (2); *Don Giovanni* (2); Exsultate, jubilate; 2 Concert Arias
Decca 443 452-2

BERGONZI, Carlo, *tenor* (b. 1924, Italy)

If Caruso made the gramophone, the gramophone made Bergonzi. There was never any question of Bergonzi's excellence in even the biggest theatres. He was the Italian tenor *par excellence*, starting with a beautiful voice and concentrating totally on perfecting his technique. Not for him the mannerisms, sobs or vocal quirks which have given so many tenors a bad name. Bergonzi never ventured outside the Italian repertoire, but in that field he was quite possibly the most reliable tenor ever to record complete operas. In the theatre he failed as an actor or great personality, but his legacy of recordings is prodigious both in numbers and in quality. Like many great tenors, he started life as a baritone and the evenness of his vocal range from the lowest to the highest register is quite remarkable. Particularly in Verdi, Bergonzi is the very model of a modern tenor-general, but he also had the required *dolcezza* to sing Puccini or Cilea with equal effect. Any set featuring this tenor has a head start.

'Carlo Bergonzi': *Aida, Luisa Miller* (Verdi), *Forza del destino, Trovatore, Ballo in maschera, Africana* (Meyerbeer), *Andrea Chénier, Adriana Lecouvreur, Tosca, Manon Lescaut, Don Carlos, Bohème, Gioconda*
Decca 440 417-2

BJÖRLING, Jussi, *tenor* (1911–1960, Sweden)

The only one of the great singers of the past who is represented several times in this book. Björling reached instant fame in the thirties, having sung in public since early childhood in a vocal quartet with his father and two brothers. He was truly a great singer, justly admired for his fine musicianship and artistic integrity. Björling had a metallic edge to his voice, unlike the then fashionable Italians, but he had the ability to sing pianissimo without any loss of quality, enlarging his repertoire of emotional light and shade vastly beyond that of competitors like the stentorian Giovanni Martinelli, yet never slipping into the crooning style of Gigli. Like Caruso, Björling died unexpectedly before reaching fifty, yet he made a number of complete opera recordings. They are so good that the mono *Bohème* in which he appears still sells readily at the full price, is worth the money and is rated the best in many CD guides!

'Opera Arias Vol. 1': *Elisir d'amore, Trovatore, Ballo in maschera, Aida, Pagliacci, Bohème* (2) (with Anne-Lise Björling), *Tosca, Fanciulla del West, Turandot, Fedora* (Giordano), *L'arlesiana* (Cilea), *Africana* (Meyerbeer), *Faust, Manon, Martha, Stabat Mater* (Rossini)
EMI CDH7 61053-2

'Björling Vol. 1': *Tosca* (2), *Bohème, Aida, Trovatore* (2), *Rigoletto* (2), *Pagliacci, Cavalleria rusticana, Fanciulla del West, Sadko* (Rimsky-Korsakov), *Africana* (Meyerbeer), *Gioconda, Manon, Stabat Mater* (Rossini), *Requiem* (Verdi), 4 Swedish songs
Nimbus NI 7835

CABALLÉ, Montserrat, *soprano* (b. 1933, Spain)

Growing up in poverty during the Spanish Civil War, Caballé learnt her craft the hard way, slogging around Swiss opera houses for nearly ten years before bursting onto the international scene in the mid-sixties, a fully fledged major star whose career is still in full flight after her sixty-second birthday! Paradoxically sporting a large lyric voice, instead of the traditional small canary, Caballé is following the great Spanish tradition of diminuendo, the ability to reduce the voice to a mere whisper of beautiful tone without any change of texture; floating top notes have made her famous and forcing the voice is not in her vocabulary. She is a musical singer who never allows her immense lung power to overshadow the composer's true intentions. Her long career has had many interruptions through illnesses, but none have affected her voice. No stranger to controversy, she never strayed from the path of producing the best in performance terms and her many complete opera recordings are universally good.

'Eternal Caballé': *Adriana Lecouvreur, Carmen, Rigoletto, Gianni Schicchi, Lucrezia Borgia* (Donizetti), *Norma, Louise, Traviata, Samson and Delilah, Roberto Devereux* (Donizetti), *Anna Bolena* (Donizetti), *Maria Stuarda* (Donizetti), *Cid* (Massenet), Spanish songs
BMG/RCA RD 61044 (2 CDs)

'Montserrat Caballé Sings Bellini & Donizetti': *Anna Bolena, Lucrezia Borgia, Maria di Rohan, Norma, Il Pirata, Roberto Devereux*
BMG/RCA 09026-61458-2

Callas

CALLAS, Maria, *soprano* (1923–1977, USA)

The most famous, but also the most infamous, prima donna of the century. No record collection is complete without at least one Callas recording, yet nothing written, other than publicity blurbs, has ever failed to criticise some aspect of her art. Callas was primarily a great singing actress endowed with a magnificent voice, which she unfortunately did not cherish as other, less important, singers have done. The many public scandals of her life should not influence a judgement of her artistry. Her performances were dramatically so electrifying that the occasional wobble or shriek was gladly forgiven by huge numbers of critics and audiences. The fact that she allowed her faults to be released in record form is the great mystery of Callas. Re-takes are the norm in recording studios and there can be little doubt that she could have eliminated at least the most glaring of her faults in her later recordings. In the early ones her weaknesses were only minor; the Callas/Di Stefano/Gobbi *Tosca* seems unlikely to be bettered. However, a huge number of later discs, recitals and complete opera recordings contain these aberrations which Callas fans take in their stride. The lady had a magnetic personality and she was able to sweep people off their feet—but not everybody. The important thing to remember about Callas is that not everything she does is perfect; far from it. If you are willing to accept her failings, she can be a most rewarding artist, but if pure vocalism is your major concern, Callas needs to be treated with great care. Some of her best complete opera recordings are recommended in this book. I have tried to offer two recitals which give a fair approximation of Callas at her best. There are dozens of others which really should be heard before purchase.

'Opera Arias': *Adriana Lecouvreur* (2), *Andrea Chénier, Wally, Mefistofele, Barber of Seville, Dinorah* (Meyerbeer), *Lakmé, Vespri Siciliani* (Verdi), *Medea* (Cherubini), *La Vestale* (Spontini) (3)
EMI CDC7 47282-2

'Mad Scenes and Bel Canto Arias': *Hamlet* (Thomas), *Anna Bolena* (Donizetti), *Lucrezia Borgia* (Donizetti), *Elisir d'amore, Daughter of the Regiment, Pirata* (Bellini)
EMI CDC7 47283

CARRERAS, José, *tenor* (b. 1946, Spain)

Possibly the most loved, but also the least important, of the 'Big Three', Carreras, Domingo and Pavarotti. (The order is always alphabetical.) Carreras started his career in spectacular fashion in the seventies as a lyric tenor and the recordings he made then will surely survive for many years to come. What brought Carreras into the big league next to his superior colleagues was a misfortune with which not only his fans, but the press empathised: he was stricken by luekemia at a crucial point of his career. The question of whether Carreras would survive, let alone sing again, made world-wide headlines. He did recover to sing again and he is such a generous and personally lovable person, whose good deeds have multiplied over the years, that it is very hard to face the reality that he is not in the same class as his two colleagues. Carreras remains among the top tenors of the world, but began to sing parts which were too heavy for him and the voice suffered as a result. There is nothing wrong with liking Carreras as he is today, but the looks and behaviour of the man should not blind CD buyers to his failings. Any Carreras CD can be enjoyed, but some are very much better than others. Those in this book are qualified where necessary.

'The Essential Carreras': *Bohème, Manon Lescaut, Turandot, Tosca, Pagliacci, Elisir d'amore, Lucia di Lammermoor, Trovatore, Luisa Miller* (Verdi), *West Side Story*, Panis Angelicus (Franck), O sole mio, Core 'ngrato, A vucchella, Mattinata, etc.
Philips 432 692-2

'Arias and Duets': *Aida* (2) (with Freni), *Don Carlos* (3) (with Cappuccilli & Freni), *Cavalleria rusticana* (3), *Pagliacci, Turandot* (2), *La Périchole* (Offenbach) (4) (with Berganza)
EMI CDM7 63111-2

DEL MONACO, Mario, *tenor* (1915–1982, Italy)

We no longer speak of male performers as matinee idols, but that description fitted Mario del Monaco like a glove. He looked like an Italian film star and acted like one. He was even elegantly slim in figure. Yet the voice which issued from this visually charming figure was not smoothly romantic; it was truly stentorian. Del Monaco trumpeted his music in heroic fashion and it must be admitted that, while he lacked subtlety, he was always on the note and without any kind of vocal flaws. Unfortunately, opera also demands a degree of charm on occasion and the voice of Del Monaco had little of that. Contrary to what has been written about him, he was not able to sing only fortissimo or forte. Some of his recorded arias prove that he was capable of singing softly, but chose not to do so most of the time. Unlike some of his Italian colleagues he satisfied his ego by bringing home the magnificence of his powerful voice without any special showmanship. Confident in his God-given instrument, he had no need to throw his weight around. On disc his penetrating voice can become tiresome; you lose the benefit of his looks and personality, but in the right parts the simple grandeur of his voice can be very impressive.

'Mario del Monaco': *Aida, Forza del destino, Ernani, Ballo in maschera, Trovatore, Otello, Gioconda, Tosca, Madama Butterfly, Turandot, Fanciulla del West, Fedora* (Giordano), *Andrea Chénier, Africana* (Meyerbeer) *Pagliacci*, O sole mio, Granada, Torna a Surriento
Decca 440 407-2

'Mario del Monaco': *Aida, Otello* (4), *Pagliacci* (2), *Turandot, Cavalleria rusticana* (2), *Andrea Chénier* (3), *Manon Lescaut, Adriana Lecouvreur* (2), *Carmen, Werther, Lohengrin, Marta, Amico Fritz* (Mascagni), *Africana* (Meyerbeer), *Bohème* (Leoncavallo)
Testament SBT 1039

DE LOS ANGELES, Victoria, *soprano* (b. 1923, Spain)

One of the most beloved of all operatic personalities, this soprano was, and still is, a major star purely on the strength of her art. So uneventful has been her life (apart from thunderous applause) that she might well be overlooked by history, were it not for the magnificent recordings she has made over the years. Prim and proper she may have been, but the music she chose to sing was at all times admirably suited to her temperament. As a result, most of her CDs and LPs are vocally close to perfection. There may have been a lack of fireworks, but even in as gross a part as Carmen, De los Angeles made you feel that she was just right for the role. Her career in the opera house was limited by her own choice, but it coincided with the introduction of stereophonic recordings. At the age of seventy she is still appearing in the venue of her choice, the concert hall, where she need sing only what lies right for her voice at any given moment. Yet her operatic recordings continue to be among the most highly recommended in current CD catalogues. A faultless artist and a beautiful voice.

'Opera Arias': *Ernani, Otello, Bohème, Mefistofele, Cenerentola, Cavalleria rusticana, Wally, Marriage of Figaro, Tannhäuser, Lohengrin, Manon, Faust*
EMI CDH7 63495-2

'Zarzuela Arias'
EMI CDM7 69078-2

DI STEFANO, Giuseppe, *tenor* (b. 1921, Italy)

The tenor who started life with a voice which promised to bring him fame as the logical successor to Caruso and Gigli did make a big name for himself—for a while. Di Stefano at his best was indeed one of the most famous tenors in the world—for a while. Like other tenors before and after him, he tackled parts which were too heavy for him and the once golden tones became dry and uninspiring. Today Di Stefano is best remembered as the partner (and probably lover) of Callas, but we have the records to prove what might have been. Unfortunately, even the best of his complete opera recordings are not as good as the arias he recorded earlier in his career. Nevertheless, enough good ones are left to make his inclusion in the book inevitable. The point to remember is that Di Stefano's best only lasted a short time—ten years at the most. His faults may not have been as bad as those of Callas, but he could not compete with her in artistry or personality.

'Opera Arias': *Mignon, Pearl Fishers, Manon, Traviata, Forza del destino, Tosca, Fanciulla del West, Gianni Schicchi, Turandot, L'arlesiana* (Cilea)
EMI CDM7 63105-2

'Operatic Arias': *Andrea Chénier, Tosca, Turandot, Carmen, Mefistofele, Elisir d'amore, Werther, Manon, Pearl Fishers, Faust, Gioconda, Forza del destino*
Decca 440 403-2

DOMINGO, Plácido, *tenor* (b. 1941, Spain)

Pavarotti may be top dog in the tenor field publicity-wise, but Domingo is a phenomenon; a tenor who is also a serious musician is a rarity indeed. Domingo may not be the greatest conductor in the world, but he can hold his own in good company, ready to make a new career when his singing days are over. He is also a first-class actor vocally as well as visually, giving his multiple recordings of operas a special meaning; his third Otello on CD is also his best. Well into his fifties, his voice shows no signs of deterioration and his innate intelligence will ensure that he will not sing music with which he can no longer ensure complete listener satisfaction. Any listed set featuring Domingo can be bought with complete confidence by a newcomer to the medium.

'The Best of Domingo': *Aida, Rigoletto, Turandot, Luisa Miller* (Verdi), *Ballo in maschera* (2), *Traviata, Carmen, Martha, Elisir d'amore, Tales of Hoffmann*
DG 415 366-2

'Bravissimo Domingo Vol. 2': *Rigoletto* (2), *Vespri Siciliani* (Verdi), *Trovatore, Luisa Miller* (Verdi), *Forza del destino, Tosca, Bohème, Norma, Cavalleria rusticana, Lohengrin, Werther, Elisir d'amore, Eugene Onegin, Martha, Andrea Chénier*
RCA 07863-56211

FRENI, Mirella, *soprano* (b. 1935, Italy)

Although this soprano does not enjoy the superstar image of Pavarotti & Co (there has never been a 'Three Sopranos Concert' which has caught the public's attention) Mirella Freni is the soprano equivalent of Pavarotti and her records number nearly as many as those of her tenor colleague; she has made more than one complete recording of many operas and not, as in the case of Tebaldi, because the first was mono and a stereo version was wanted. Like most sopranos, Freni started in the lyric field and then graduated to heavier parts as she grew older. Another parallel with Pavarotti is the fact that her most recent recordings are not as good as her earlier ones; she turned sixty this year! I have taken this fact into consideration in this book.

'Opera': *Adriana Lecouvreur, Gianni Schicchi, Marriage of Figaro, Puritani, Traviata, Carmen, Pearl Fishers, Manon, Rondine, Tosca, Manon Lescaut, Turandot, Madama Butterfly, Suor Angelica, Louise* (Charpentier)
EMI CDM7 63110-2

'Operatic Arias': *Bohème, Tosca, Madama Butterfly, Falstaff, Pagliacci, Mefistofele, William Tell* (Rossini), *Bianca e Fernando* (Bellini), *Ninnananna* (Pratella)
Decca 440 412-2

GEDDA, Nicolai, *tenor* (b. 1925, Sweden)

Nicolai Ustinov (a distant relative of Sir Peter) became one of the world's most versatile tenors under the stage name of Gedda. Fluent in eight languages and in every conceivable type of music, Gedda's voice can be exceptionally beautiful in just about anything he attempts. His Rodolfo in *La bohème* opposite Mirella Freni's first Mimì can hold its own against almost all comers; for years only Gedda attempted the fiendish role of Arnold in Rossini's *William Tell;* and he was the worthy partner of Elisabeth Schwarzkopf in the most successful series of operetta recordings ever made. He is still recording minor roles which are suited to the personality of a seventy-year-old, for example several cameos in Bernstein's *Candide*. His name appears frequently in this book. Look out for it; he is a very positive asset to anything he does. Unfortunately, there are no full recital discs of his voice at present, though he inevitably appears in highlights and mixed recital CDs.

GOBBI, Tito, *baritone* (1913–1984, Italy)

The most important baritone ever to make records, even though he did not have the greatest voice of the century. Gobbi personified the ideal opera singer in vocal, musical and acting terms. The fact that his voice was not big enough to rattle the rafters did not stop him from being a major attraction in the theatre. On disc that minor shortcoming disappears completely. Here is one singer whose every record will give unalloyed pleasure. There are no mannerisms, an immense variety of vocal colours and certainly no forcing or loss of control, let alone excessive vibrato.

Gobbi

'Opera Arias': *Fanciulla del West, Andrea Chénier, Nabucco, Elisir d'amore, Ballo in maschera, Otello, Marriage of Figaro, Forza del destino, Don Carlos, Zazà* (Leoncavallo), *L'arlesiana* (Cilea), etc.
EMI CDM7 63109-2

'Tito Gobbi': *Don Giovanni, Don Carlos, Fanciulla del West, Barber of Seville, Pagliacci, Otello, Marriage of Figaro, Traviata, Rigoletto, Macbeth, O sole mio, Santa Lucia, A vucchella, Marechiare* & 6 other songs
Testament SBT 1019

HORNE, Marilyn, *mezzo-soprano* (b. 1934, USA)

Many mezzo-sopranos try to become fully fledged sopranos, but never with increased success. Marilyn Horne's spectacular career has remained in the mezzo field. A hundred years ago she might well have been classed as a contralto; she certainly has the chest register of the older singers, as well as their agility. No Rossini mezzos today have the power, volume and velvety sound of Horne, and she excels in much more than just that field; she is in a class of her own and, unlike her tenor and soprano colleagues, she does not re-record parts unless she can improve on earlier performances. The name Marilyn Horne on any playbill guarantees great singing.

'Arias': *Barber of Seville, Semiramide* (2), *Lucrezia Borgia, Cenerentola, Daughter of the Regiment, Italiana in Algeri* (Rossini) (2), *Capuleti e i Montechi* (Bellini)
Decca 421 891-2

'Operatic Arias': *Semele, Carmen, Samson and Delilah, Rodelinda* (Handel), *Clemenza di Tito* (Mozart), *Alceste* (Gluck), *Italiana in Algeri* (Rossini), *Sapho* (Gounod), *Donna del lago* (Rossini), etc.
Decca 440 415-2

NILSSON, Birgit, *soprano* (b. 1928, Sweden)

One of the greatest of the Scandinavian singers—you can't call her 'the' greatest, when you consider Kirsten Flagstad, Jussi Björling, Lauritz Melchior and the like—Nilsson had a voice of steel which could cut through the thickest of Wagnerian orchestrations like a knife, yet hold its own in the Italian repertoire as well; her Turandot was unequalled in her time and her Tosca not lightly dismissed. But Wagner was her forte; unfortunately, she lived in an age when male Wagnerian singers were in short supply. She does not appear as often in this book as she should, being let down by colleagues whose contribution to complete opera recordings must be taken into consideration. Nilsson appears in most collections of great sopranos or great singers of the century and, of course, in innumerable highlights from Wagner operas, but there are few, if any, Nilsson solo recitals of arias available on CD.

'Public Performances 1954–1969': *Lohengrin, Tristan und Isolde, Walküre, Tosca, Turandot*, 3 Schubert songs, 4 Richard Strauss Songs (with Windgassen, Varnay, Vickers, Domingo, Corelli, Uhde)
Memories HR 4275/6 (2 CDs)

NORMAN, Jessye, *soprano* (b. 1945, USA)

Here is a big singer indeed. A giant of a woman with a gigantic voice, which she uses in a most musical manner. On disc her size (tall as well as wide) is unimportant; her superb vocalism and musicality are impeccable. Possibly because she overshadows all others on stage, her career is largely aimed at the concert platform, but this in no way interferes with complete opera recordings. She produces a beautiful sound, soaring effortlessly over the largest orchestra.

'Scenes from Wagner': *Tristan und Isolde, Flying Dutchman, Götterdämmerung, Tannhäuser* (2)
EMI CDC7 49759-2

'L'Incomparable': *Belle Hélène* (Offenbach), *Euryanthe* (Weber), *Romeo and Juliet* (Berlioz), *German Requiem* (Brahms), Wesendonck Lieder (Wagner), Chansons medécasses (Ravel)
EMI CDM7 69256-2

PAVAROTTI, Luciano, *tenor* (b. 1935, Italy)

Probably the most famous tenor since Caruso, thanks to a carefully prepared world-wide publicity campaign (a man called Herbert Breslin actually wrote a self-promoting book, telling how he did it) Pavarotti fortunately does not disappoint. The voice was always superb and his first-class records so numerous that his fame is well-justified, even though he can be accused, as Beniamino Gigli was, of playing to the gallery—or should that be the stadium these days? Sixty in 1995, it is perhaps regrettable that he is still making records, since they cannot possibly be as good as those he made twenty years earlier. Pavarotti has recorded everything he has ever sung and is ever likely to sing. His second *Pagliacci* is simply not as good as his first. Yet, had he not made the first recording, the later one would be considered great singing. He is far from finished, but it is wise to consider other factors than just the name Pavarotti in the case of any of his recent recordings. His existing repertoire of CDs is so good that anything new requires very close attention before purchase. This book contains only his best.

'Favourite Tenor Arias': *Pagliacci, Martha, Carmen, Bohème, Tosca, Turandot, Rigoletto, Aida, Trovatore, Faust*
Decca 400 053-2

'King of the High Cs': *Puritani, Daughter of the Regiment, Favorita, Bohème, William Tell* (Rossini), *Rosenkavalier, Trovatore*
Decca 433 437-2

PRICE, Leontyne, *soprano* (b. 1927, USA)

This great American soprano broke the colour barrier for opera singers; the token appearance of Marian Anderson at the Metropolitan hardly counted. Price is a typical Afro-American, visually suited to little other than Aida, but the quality of her singing was so high ('great' is not inapplicable) that she became a superstar, whose name ranked high at the box office anywhere, and on recordings her colour does not matter; she heads dozens of superb CD opera sets. Price was followed by an avalanche of black singers, which continues to this day. Her speciality was Verdi, though she recorded much else and any set which features her name must be very seriously considered on her contribution alone.

'Verdi Heroines': *Aida, Ballo in maschera, Ernani, Forza del destino, Macbeth, Otello, Traviata, Trovatore*
RCA 07863-57016-2

'Puccini Heroines': *Bohème, Edgar, Fanciulla del West, Gianni Schicchi, Madama Butterfly, Manon Lescaut, Rondine, Tosca, Turandot, Villi*
RCA 07863-55999-2

RAMEY, Samuel, *bass* (b. 1942, USA)

A very strange phenomenon, this: a star bass of more import at the box office than Ezio Pinza, though not yet legendary like Chaliapine. Ramey's voice is superb, his musicianship is exemplary and he has the looks of a macho Hollywood star, including a mighty chest, which he exploits to the full in many a barbaric part in which he shines on stage. On disc the latter virtues do not count, but there is no arguing with his singing; it can only be described as great. No mannerisms, no faulty intonation. A fine singer, who adds immeasurably to any recording on which he appears.

'French Opera Arias': *Carmen, Tales of Hoffmann, Faust* (3), *Siège de Corinthe* (Rossini), *Huguenots* (Meyerbeer), *Caïd* (Thomas), *Jolie fille de Perth* (Bizet), *Gisélidis* (Massenet), *Jongleur de Notre-Dame* (Massenet), *Don Quichotte* (Massenet)
Philips 432 080-2

'Rossini Arias': *Cenerentola* (3), *Semiramide, Italiana in Algeri, Stabat Mater, Viaggio a Reims*
Teldec 9031-73242-2

SCHWARZKOPF, Elisabeth, *soprano* (b. 1915, Germany)

Many great singers were born and sang in Germany. Schwarzkopf is the perfect example. Decidedly a German-trained singer, the purity of her voice compares favourably with that of most Italians of her time. The glorious heritage of recordings she

Schwarzkopf

has left for posterity looks like immortalising her forever. In this book, two of the three recommended recordings of the much-recorded *Merry Widow* star Schwarzkopf with various partners. Lehár may be easy to sing compared with other works in which Schwarzkopf is just as good. But that her mono *Widow* should survive along with her stereo one to this day reflects on the sheer beauty of her singing, not to mention her musicianship. Perhaps Schwarzkopf was pampered by her record company; after all, she married its boss, Walter Legge, also a legend in his own lifetime. But that fact did not ensure the continuing success of her recordings on CD sixteen years after his death. This singer is one of the glories of the twentieth century and she appears in many more opera sets than you will find in this book.

'Opera Arias': *Marriage of Figaro, Così fan tutte, Don Giovanni, Hänsel und Gretel, Lustige Witwe, Fledermaus, Turandot, Rosenkavalier, Ariadne auf Naxos* (R Strauss), *Capriccio* (R Strauss), Requiem (Verdi)
EMI CDM7 63657-2

'Elisabeth Schwarzkopf Sings Operetta': *Opera Ball* (Heuberger), *Vogelhändler* (Zeller) (2), *Obersteiger* (Zeller), *Zarewitsch* (Lehár), *Count of Luxemburg, Giuditta* (Lehár), *Boccaccio* (Suppé), *Dubarry* (Millöcker), Vienna, City of my dreams, etc.
EMI CDC7 47284-2

STUDER, Cheryl, *soprano* (b. 1955, USA)

The first soprano for a hundred years who not only sings every type of part, but sings them all well. Those of the past never recorded complete operas and cannot thus be compared, but no singer in recent history has been equally successful in roles as varied as Salome, the Queen of the Night, Marguerite, Elsa, Lucia di Lammermoor and even Hanna Glawari in *The Merry Widow*. Only forty this year, Studer is probably already a superstar just waiting for the tenor craze to die down. On disc she can and does tackle just about anything and no criticism of her work on stage has ever appeared. She is no Callas or Sutherland or Melba; I consider that the name Studer will probably be bandied about in a similar fashion in years to come.

'Cheryl Studer': *Faust, Don Giovanni, Sonnambula, Walküre, Mastersingers, Tristan und Isolde, Vespri Siciliani* (Verdi), *Attila* (Verdi), *Requiem* (Verdi), *Frau ohne Schatten* (R Strauss), *Elektra* (R Strauss)
EMI CDC 5 55350-2

'Coloratura': *Norma, Sonnambula, Traviata, Trovatore, Lucia di Lammermoor, Barber of Seville, Semiramide, Lucrezia Borgia (Donizetti)*
EMI CDC7 49961-2

SUTHERLAND, Joan, *soprano* (b. 1926, Australia)

A singer who, in Australia and New Zealand, needs no introduction, beyond saying that she is as famous overseas as she is at home; only Melba achieved comparable fame. The reason for Sutherland's success lay not only in the phenomenal recordings she made throughout a very long career, but in the fact that hers was, strictly speaking, a dramatic soprano and not a tiny, warbling coloratura voice. It is seldom mentioned that both she and Callas started as Wagnerians! Sutherland did not retire until well past sixty, too late, perhaps. Fortunately, most of the recordings she made during her last years were intended for the video market. The many CD sets listed in this book were made long before that time and show 'Our Joan' in all her true glory.

'Prima donna assoluta': *Tales of Hoffmann, Daughter of the Regiment, Lucia di Lammermoor, Lakmé, Faust, Puritani, Traviata, Rosamunda d'Inghilterra* (Donizetti)
Decca 425 605-2

'Italian Operatic Arias': *Norma, Puritani, Lucia di Lammermoor, Ernani, Linda di Chamounix* (Donizetti), *Attila* (Verdi), *Vespri Siciliani* (Verdi)
Decca 440 404-2

TEBALDI, Renata, *soprano* (b. 1922, Italy)

Maria Callas' supposed 'rival', Renata Tebaldi was the biggest soprano star when Callas arrived on the scene. Any rivalry there may have been was restricted to their fans, however. Their repertoire hardly overlapped. Callas was a dramatic coloratura and Tebaldi what is known as a *spinto* (Butterfly, Desdemona). Tebaldi did not have Callas' trill, Callas did not have Tebaldi's total evenness of vocal emission. Comparisons in this case are not odious, they are pointless. Tebaldi had one of the biggest and most beautiful voices ever recorded and the best of her complete recordings are available on CD, blessedly on cheaper discs. Perhaps Tebaldi was not the greatest actress, but she poured forth a glorious torrent of sound—and retired without fanfare before the voice lost its sheen. Would that all singers did the same. Unlike Callas, any Tebaldi recording can be bought without reservations, except perhaps for the fact that, although she shone brightest in the early days of LPs, those surrounding her unfortunately did not always achieve the standard she set.

'Italian Opera Arias': *Madama Butterfly, Bohème, Turandot, Tosca, Gianni Schicchi, Suor Angelica, Fanciulla del West, Manon Lescaut, Aida, Otello, Forza del destino, Adriana Lecouvreur, Andrea Chénier, Mefistofele, Wally*
Decca 440 408-2

'The Early Recordings': *Aida, Trovatore, Faust, Madama Butterfly* (2), *Manon Lescaut, Tosca, Bohème* (2), *Aida* (Act 3 with Del Monaco & Protti)
Decca 425 989-2

TE KANAWA, Kiri, *soprano* (b. 1944, New Zealand)

New Zealand's Joan Sutherland, 'Kiri' is the only female superstar in the operatic firmament these days and she has earned that position the hard way. Hers is a beautiful voice without a doubt and its individuality makes it unmistakable. Her artistic instincts are not infallible, however, and I am not speaking about her cross-over activities into the field of Cole Porter or George Gershwin. Te Kanawa never sings badly, but she has been known to record works not suited to all aspects of her talents. These do not, of course, appear in this book.

'Italian Opera Arias': *Turandot, Suor Angelica, Andrea Chénier, Pagliacci, Mefistofele, Trovatore, Traviata, Forza del destino, Adriana Lecouvreur*
EMI CDC7 54062-2

Te Kanawa

'The Essential Kiri': *Tosca, Carmen, Manon Lescaut, Otello, Marriage of Figaro* (2), Pie Jesu (Fauré), *Messiah* (Handel), Bachianas brasileiras No. 5 (Villa-Lobos), Nun's Chorus (J Strauss), *Carousel* (Rodgers), Ave Maria (Bach/Gounod), *Samson* (Handel), Vocalise (Rachmaninov), Beim Schlafengehen (R Strauss)
Decca 436286-2

THE MIXED CD
Recital

This book is a guide to complete opera recordings. However, there is a plethora of mixed recitals discs which are not only popular, but are a good guide to the type of music and the singers featured in many fine complete opera sets. A full listing of such CDs available at any given point in time would require a book in itself. The 1995 *Gramophone* catalogue contains no less than eighty-seven different single CDs featuring the voice of Plácido Domingo issued by thirteen different companies, not including highlights from any one opera!

Recitals are recycled by companies in new forms at regular intervals and the identical recordings of arias and other extracts from operas often appear on more than one CD. (Domingo did not record eighty-seven different recitals!) Those by individual singers which are listed on pages 143–163 are likely to be available for some time, but they do not stay in the catalogue as long as complete opera sets, and their availability cannot be guaranteed.

The mixed recital is the ideal introduction to opera, offering several singers in extracts from many operas. Fans of particular artists will inevitably buy CDs featuring their favourites, but even they can benefit from the following method of selecting CDs for purchase.

I have chosen the ten most popular arias, duets and ensembles in each voice range which are likely to appear on solo and mixed recital CDs. No one CD will contain all your favourites, but those I have listed cannot fail to please anyone interested in singing. Recitals on sale in any shop will contain a majority of the musical items I have chosen. Avoid single composer discs and 'rarities'. By comparing a CD's content with these lists and buying accordingly, you will obtain enjoyable listening for many years to come and a means of exploring the complete operas to which this book is devoted.

The Top Ten Tenor Arias

Bizet	*Carmen*	La fleur que tu m'avais jetée
Donizetti	*L'elisir d'amore*	Una furtiva lagrima
Leoncavallo	*Pagliacci*	Vesti la giubba
Ponchielli	*La gioconda*	Cielo e mar
Puccini	*La bohème*	Che gelida manina
Puccini	*Tosca*	E lucevan le stelle
Puccini	*Turandot*	Nessun dorma
Verdi	*Aida*	Celeste Aida
Verdi	*Rigoletto*	La donna è mobile
Verdi	*Il trovatore*	Di quella pira

The Top Ten Soprano Arias

Bellini	*Norma*	Casta diva
Catalani	*La Wally*	Ebben, ne andrò lontana
Donizetti	*Lucia di Lammermoor*	Ardon gl'incensi
Dvořák	*Rusalka*	O Silver Moon
Puccini	*La bohème*	Mi chiamano Mimì
Puccini	*Gianni Schicchi*	O mio babbino caro
Puccini	*Madama Butterfly*	Un bel di vedremo
Puccini	*Tosca*	Vissi d'arte
Verdi	*Rigoletto*	Caro nome
Verdi	*La traviata*	Ah, fors è lui

The Top Ten Baritone Arias

Bizet	*Carmen*	Votre toast
Leoncavallo	*Pagliacci*	Prologue
Mozart	*The Magic Flute*	Der Vogelfänger bin ich ja
Mozart	*Le nozze di Figaro*	Non più andrai
Rossini	*The Barber of Seville*	Largo al factotum
Verdi	*Un ballo in maschera*	Eri tu
Verdi	*Otello*	Credo
Verdi	*La traviata*	Di provenza il mar
Verdi	*Il trovatore*	Il balen
Wagner	*Tannhäuser*	O du mein holder Abendstern

The Top Ten Mezzo-soprano Arias

Bizet	*Carmen*	Habanera
Bizet	*Carmen*	Seguidilla
Donizetti	*Lucrezia Borgia*	Il segreto
Gluck	*Orpheus and Euridice*	Che farò senza Euridice
Rossini	*The Barber of Seville*	Una voce poco fa
Saint-Saëns	*Samson and Delilah*	Printemps qui commence
Saint-Saëns	*Samson and Delilah*	Mon coeur s'ouvre
Thomas	*Mignon*	Connais-tu le pays
Verdi	*Don Carlos*	O don fatale
Verdi	*Il trovatore*	Stride la vampa

The Top Ten Bass Arias

Boito	*Mefistofele*	Son lo spirito
Gounod	*Faust*	Le veau d'or
Mozart	*Die Entführung*	Wer ein Liebchen
Mozart	*The Magic Flute*	In diesen heil'gen Hallen
Mozart	*The Magic Flute*	O Isis und Osiris
Rossini	*The Barber of Seville*	La calunnia
R Strauss	*Der Rosenkavalier*	Herr Kavalier
Verdi	*Don Carlos*	Dormiro sol
Verdi	*The Sicilian Vespers*	O tu Palermo
Verdi	*Simon Boccanegra*	Il lacerato spirito

The Top Ten Operatic Ensembles

Bizet	*The Pearl Fishers*	Au fond du temple (t, b)
Donizetti	*Lucia di Lammermoor*	Chi mi frena
Mozart	*Don Giovanni*	La ci darem (b, s)
Offenbach	*Tales of Hoffmann*	Barcarolle (s, ms)
Puccini	*La bohème*	O soave fanciulla (t, s)
Verdi	*Forza del destino*	Solenne in quest'ora (t, b)
Verdi	*Rigoletto*	Bella figlia dell'amore
Verdi	*Il trovatore*	Miserere (t, s)
Verdi	*Il trovatore*	Ai nostri monti (t, ms)

The Mixed CD Recital

Like the recitals listed for individual singers, the following CDs are likely to be available in the foreseeable future, but these also may be withdrawn and parts re-issued in different combinations.

'A Night at the Opera Vol. 1: Puccini Gala': *Bohème, Madama Butterfly, Turandot, Tosca, Manon Lescaut, Gianni Schicchi, Rondine*
Caballé, Carreras, Domingo, Freni, Te Kanawa, Pavarotti, Tebaldi, Milnes, Ludwig
Decca 440 072-2

'A Night at the Opera Vol. 2: Duets': *Otello, Lakmé, Traviata, Semiramide, Bohème, Rigoletto, Marriage of Figaro, Don Giovanni, Pearl Fishers, Cavalleria rusticana, Barber of Seville, Tosca, Hänsel und Gretel, Der Rosenkavalier* (R Strauss), *Arabella* (R Strauss)
L Price–Di Stefano, Te Kanawa–Popp, Popp–Fassbaender, Pavarotti–Te Kanawa, Sutherland–Berbié, Sutherland–Pavarotti, Cross–Quilico, Sutherland–Horne, Bergonzi–Bastianini, Bergonzi–Nucci, Pavarotti–Anderson, Pavarotti–Varady, Te Kanawa–Fontana, Gueden–Söderstrom, Popp–Krause
Decca 440 203-2

'A Night at the Opera Vol. 3: Mozart Gala': *Don Giovanni, Così fan tutte, Marriage of Figaro, Magic Flute, Re Pastore, Seraglio*
Te Kanawa, Bartoli, Popp, Jo, Weikl, Lorengar, Prey, Burrows, Talvela, Weikl, Ramey, Krause, Berganza, Heilmann, Moll, Gruberová, Battle, etc.
Decca 440 591-2

'A Night at the Opera Vol. 4: Great Italian Opera': *Pagliacci, Cavalleria rusticana, Bohème, Rigoletto, Tosca, Macbeth, Barber of Seville, Lucia di Lammermoor, Madama Butterfly, Cenerentola, L'arlesiana* (Cilea)
Sutherland, Bartoli, Te Kanawa, Berganza, Pavarotti, Carreras, Fischer-Dieskau, Nucci, G Evans, L Price, Freni, Varady, Aragall, etc.
Decca 440 592-2

The Good Opera CD Guide

'Opera's Greatest Moments': *Traviata, Gianni Schicchi, Barber of Seville, Pearl Fishers, Bohème, Wally, Elisir d'amore, Walküre, Forza del destino, Pagliacci, Marriage of Figaro, Rigoletto, Madama Butterfly, Magic Flute, Aida, Carmen, Turandot, Queen of Spades* (Tchaikovsky)
Moffo, Donath, Caballé, Marton, Norman, Price, Varady, Cotrubas, Berganza, Tucker, Björling, Domingo, Kraus, Lanza, Heppner, Merrill, Hvorostovsky
RCA 09026-61440-2

'Greatest Love Songs': *Carmen, Marriage of Figaro, Martha, Madama Butterfly, Aida, Traviata, Tosca* (2), *Bohème, Magic Flute, Turandot, Rigoletto, Romeo and Juliet, Tristan und Isolde, Chérubin* (Massenet)
Corelli, Varady, Domingo, Moffo, Björling, Caballé, Pavarotti, Tucker, Upshaw, L Price, M Price, Tappy
RCA 09026-61886-2

'Duets': *Don Giovanni, Barber of Seville, Trovatore, Boris Godounov, Andrea Chénier, Pearl Fishers, Madama Butterfly, Tosca, Bohème*
Callas–Gobbi, Callas–Bergonzi, Corelli–Tucci, Corelli–Stella, Gedda–Freni, Gedda–Blanc, Waechter–Sciutti, Björling–De los Angeles, Lear–Uzounov
Classics for Pleasure CDB 762023-2

'The Best of Opera Vol. 2': *Bohème, Madam Butterfly, Traviata, Magic Flute, Tales of Hoffmann, Tosca, Barber of Seville, Wally, Cosi fan tutte, Marriage of Figaro, Manon Lescaut, Carmen, Rigoletto, Aida, Gioconda, Orpheus and Euridice* Gauci, Ramiro, Miricioiu, Kaludov, Servile, Tichy, Borowsky, etc.
Naxos 8.553167

New release by ABC Classics in April 1996:
'Thirty Years of Singers of Renown'
The best arias, duets, etc. chosen from Australia's longest running radio program presented on Radio National by the author of this book, John Cargher. Details not yet available.

Index of Artists

Italics indicate additional textual inclusion.
Major entries are marked *.

b = baritone
ba = bass
c = conductor
ct = counter-tenor
ms = mezzo-soprano
s = soprano
t = tenor

Abbado, Claudio, c 27, 80, 122, 126, 130, *135*
Abbado, Roberto, c 35
Ackermann, Otto, c 59, 61, 111
Adam, Theo, ba 136, 139, 140
Adams, Donald, ba 116, 117
Adrian, Max, b 24
Agache, Alexandru, b 38, 47
Ainsley, John Mark, t 67, 117
Alagna, Roberto, t 36, *37*
Alaimo, Simone, b 104
Alarie, Pierette, s 28
Albert, Donnie Ray, ba 43
Aler, John, t 28, 53
Alexander, John, t 21
Allen, Thomas, b 35, 47, 71, 74, 78, 115, 117, 118
Allers, Franz, c 67, 72
Almeida, Antonio de, c 50
Alva, Luigi, t 51, 75, 102
Amara, Lucine, s 85
Anders, Peter, t 41
Anderson, June, s 24, *50*, 167
Anderson, Marian, ms *158*

Andreas, Christine, s 98
Andrews, Julie, s *68*, 96, *97, 99*
Anheisser, Wolfgang, b 56
Anisimov, Alexander, ba 118
Aragall, Giacomo, t 130, 167
Araiza, Francisco, t 32, 74, 79, 82, *83*, 104
Argenta, Nancy, s 46
Arié, Rafael, ba 38
Arroyo, Martina, s 125
Ashe, Rosemary, s 101
Augér, Arleen, s 51, 77
Ayars, Ann, s 46
Ayldon, John, ba 116, 117

Bacquier, Gabriel, b 34, 35, 82
Bailey, Norman, b 101
Baker, George, b *115*
Baker, Janet, ms *46, 52*, 74
Balslev, Lisbeth, s 134
Baltsa, Agnes, ms 27, *28*, 75, 83, 104, 106, *107*, 113, 120, 122, 137, *138*
Bär, Olaf, b 79, 109
Barbaux, Christine, s 71
Barber, Lynn, s 56
Barbieri, Fedora, ms 94, 120, 124, 132
Barbirolli, John, c 88, *89*
Barioni, Daniele, t *91*
Barrett, Brent, b 67
Barstow, Josephine, s 84, *85*, 121
Bartoletti, Bruno, c 83
Bartoli, Cecilia, ms *102, 104*, 147*
Barton, Steve, b 64
Bastianini, Ettore, b 44, 69, 85, 167

169

Index of Artists

Battle, Kathleen, s 36, 53, *102*, 121, 167
Beckerbauer, Stefan, treble 46
Beecham, Sir Thomas, c 27, *28*, *48*, 85, *86*
Begg, Heather, ms 116
Behrens, Hildegard, s 54, *113*, 134, *140*
Bellezza, Vincenzo, c 94
Bell, Marion, s 67
Benacková, Gabriella, s *40*, *108*
Berbié, Jane, ms 34, 167
Berger, Erna, s 41
Berganza, Teresa, ms 27, 51, 151, 167, 168
Bergonzi, Carlo, t *33*, 63, 70, 83, 85, 88, 120, 121, 123, *125*, 148*, 156, 167, 168
Bernius, Frieder, c 46
Bernstein, Leonard, c 24, *25*, *26*, *124*, 155
Berry, Walter, b 20, 108, 138
Bianco, René, b 28
Bikel, Theodore, b 96, *97*, 99
Björling, Anne-Lise, s 149
Björling, Jussi, t 28, *41*, 69, 85, *86*, 88, 120, 132, *133*, 148*, 156, 168
Blackton, Jay, c 98
Blackwell, Harolyn, s 43
Blake Jones, Philip, t 116
Blanc, Ernest, b 27, 47, 106, 168
Blochwitz, Hans-Peter, t 74
Blyth, Ann, s 101
Boehm, see Böhm
Böhm, Karl, c 74, 77, 138, *139*
Böhm, Karl-Walter, t, 113
Böhme, Kurt, ba 59
Bonney, Barbara, s 54, *61*, 79
Bonynge, Richard, c 21, 22, 23, 33, 34, 36, 37, 38, 47, 51, 82, 105, 129, 131
Borg, Kim, b 80
Boskovsky, Willi, c 59, 111

Bottone, Bonaventura, t 101, 116
Bowman, James, ct 52
Braun, Victor, b 137
Brightman, Sarah, s 64
Britton, Pamela, ms 67
Bronhill, June, s 61
Brooks, David, b 67
Brownlee, John, b 146
Bruscantini, Sesto, b 35, 104
Bruson, Renato, b 35, *36*, 90, 121, 123, 124, 125, 126, 129
Bryant, Jim, t 26
Brynner, Yul, b 96, *97*
Bumbry, Grace, ms 137
Burchuladze, Paata, ba 102, 118, 125, 130
Burgess, Sally, s 57
Burles, Charles, t 34
Burrowes, Norma, ms 53
Burrows, Stuart, t 118, 167
Bychkov, Semyon, c 118

Caballé, Montserrat, s *22*, 29, 44, *45*, 63, 74, 83, *84*, 95, 120, 122, 149*, 167, 168
Cachamaille, Gilles, b 79
Callas, Maria, s *21*, *22*, 23, *24*, 38, *39*, 69, 83, *84*, *86*, *89*, *92*, *102*, *129*, *132*, *133*, 150*, *161*, *162*, 168
Cambreling, Phillipe, c 82
Campbell, Elizabeth, ms 52
Campora, Giuseppe, t 130
Canonici, Luca, t 35
Cappuccilli, Piero, b 22, 83, 120, 122, 125, *126*, *127*, *130*, 151
Capuana, Franco, c 33, 87
Carlyle, Joan, s 63
Carreras, José, t *8*, 26, 27, *28*, *50*, 71, 72, 92, *93*, *100*, 106, *107*, *120*, 122, *125*, 126, *130*, 151*, 167
Caruso, Enrico, t, *8*, *33*, *41*, *50*, 87, *88*, *132*, *143*, 143*, *145*, *148*. *153*, *158*
Cava, Carlo, ba 127
Cellini, Renato, c 132

Index of Artists

Chailly, Riccardo, c 44, 104
Chakaris, George, b 26
Chance, Michael, ct 46, 53
Charisse, Cyd, s 67
Chernov, Vladimir, b 132, *133*
Christoff, Boris, ba *30*, 47, *48*, 80, *81*, *123*, *130*
Chung, Myung-Whun, c 106, 128
Cioni, Renato, t *39*
Ciurca, Cleopatra, ms 33
Clayton, Jan, s 57
Cleva, Fausto, c 32
Cluytens, André, c 47, *48*
Coburn, Pamela, s 20, 111
Collier, Marie, s 88
Connell, Elizabeth, s 118
Cook, Barbara, s 24, 96, *97*
Corbelli, Claude, b 104
Corelli, Franco, t 47, 95, *96*, 157, 168,
Corena, Fernando, ba *36*, 94
Cossa, Dominic, b 36
Cossotto, Fiorenza, ms 78, 83, 120, 126, 132
Cotrubas, Ileana, s 27, 28, 36, *37*, 70, 94, 131, *132*, 168
Craig, Charles, t 88
Crawford, Michael, b 64, *65*
Creasy, Philip, t 117
Crespin, Régine, s *112*, *113*, 139
Criswell, Kim, ms 84
Croft, Dwayne, b 90
Cross, Richard, ba 21, 167

d'Angelo, Gianna, s 85
d'Arcangelo, Ildebrando, ba 75
Dalberg, Friedrich, ba 136
Dale, Clamma, s 43
Dalton, Andrew, ct 52
Danieli, Elena, s 29
Dara, Enzo, b 36, 104
Davenport, Pembroke, c 84
Davies, Joan, ms 117
Davies, Maldwyn, t 51

Davis, Colin, c 54, 71, *72*, 74, 78, 106
Dawson, Lynne, s 75, *76*
De Grandis, Franco, ba 102
De Gutzman, Josie, s 66
De los Angeles, Victoria, s 27, *28*, 47, *48*, 70, *71*, *72*, 85, *86*, 88, 94, *130*, 152*, 168
De Palma, Piero, t 91
De Sabata, Victor, c 92
Del Monaco, Mario, t 29, 32, *33*, 44, *45*, *87*, 94, *128*, 151*, 162
Del Monte, Carlo, t 94
DeMain, John, c 43
Dens, Michel, b 70
Depraz, Xavier, ba 70
Dernesch, Helga, s 20, 137, 138, *139*
Devia, Mariella, s 36
Di Stasio, Anna, ms 88
Di Stefano, Giuseppe, t 22, 38, 69, *92*, *93*, *129*, *133*, 150, 153*, 167
Díaz, Justino, ba, 128
Dimitrova, Ghena, s *127*
Dobrowen, Issay, c 80
Dohnányi, Christoph von, c 134
Domingo, Plácido, t *8*, 27, 29, *30*, 33, 36, *37*, 38, *39*, *41*, 44, 45, 47, 63, *64*, 69, *72*, *82*, *83*, *87*, *90*, *91*, *92*, *93*, 94, 95, *102*, 106, *107*, *109*, *120*, 121, 122, 123, *125*, 126, 127, *128*, *130*, 131, *132*, *133*, 135, *136*, 137, *138*, 151, 154*, 164, 167, 168
Domingo, Plácido, c 109
Donath, Helen, s 20, 59, 94, 112, 136, 168
Dowling, Dennis, b 116
Drake, Alfred, b 84, *85*
Ducarel, Michael, ba 116
Dunn, Vivian, c 117
Dvonch, Frederick, c 99
Dvorsky, Peter, t *108*

Eaglen, Jane, s 21
Eddy, Nelson, b *98*
Edelmann, Otto, ba 112, 136

171

Index of Artists

Edwards, John Owen, c 26, 57, 101, 117
Eisler, David, t 24
Elvira, Pablo, b 69
Engel, Lehmann, c 98
Erede, Alberto, c 49, 69, 85
Estes, Simon, b 134
Evans Geraint, b 36, *115*, 167
Evans, Rebecca, s 115, 117

Faris, Alexander, c 116
Fassbaender, Brigitte, ms 41, 109, 129, 132, 167
Ferraro, Pier Miranda, t 83
Ferrier, Kathleen, ms 46
Ferrin, Agostino, ba 22
Ferro, Gabriele, c 35
Fieldsend, David, t 115, 117
Fillipeschi, Mario, t 21
Fink, Bernarda, s 52
Finke, Martin, t 73
Fioravante, Giulio, b 33
Fischer-Dieskau, Dietrich, b 111, *124*, 135, *136*, 138, 167
Flagello, Ezio, ba 51, 123
Flagstad, Kirsten, s *21*, 138, *139*, *156*
Focile, Nuccia, s 118
Fondary, Alain, b 87, 106
Fontana, Gabriele, s 167
Fournet, Jean, c 28
Fournier, Brigitte, s 46
Fredericks, Charles, t 57
Freni, Mirella, s 29, 35, 47, 51, 63, 78, 85, 88, *89*, *90*, *92*, *93*, *94*, 118, 120, 120, 122, 123, 125, 130, 151, 154*, 167, 168
Frick, Gottlob, ba 20, 108, 135
Fuchs, Gabriele, s 73
Furlanetto, Ferrucio, ba 50, 75
Furtwängler, Wilhelm, c 138, *139*

Gabarain, Marina de, ms 104
Gähmlich, Wilfried, t 77
Gale, Elizabeth, s 46

Gallagher, Peter, b 66
Galliera, Alceo, c 102
Ganassi, Sonia, s 102
Ganzarolli, Wladimiro, b 74, 78
Gardelli, Lamberto, c 83, 94, 125, 127
Gardiner, John Eliot, c 46, *53*, *61*, 75, 77, 78
Gasdia, Cecilia, s 47
Gauci, Miriam, s 63, 90, 168
Gavazzeni, Gianandrea, c 44
Gaynor, Mitzi, s 100
Gedda, Nicolai, t 27, 41, 47, 56, 59, *60*, 61, 71, 72, 74, 80, 109, *111*, 155*, 168
Gelmetti, Gianluigi, c 102
Ghiaurov, Nicolai, ba 22, 23, 29, *30*, 38, 47, 80, *81*, 83, 118, 122, 123, 130
Ghiuselev, Nicolai, ba 83
Giaiotti, Bonaldo, ba 125, 132
Gigli, Beniamino, t *45*, *147*, *148*, *153*, *158*
Gilfry, Rodney, b 75, 78
Gillett, Christopher, t 115
Giménez, Raúl, t *102*, 104
Giulini, Carlo Maria, c 75, 78, 122, 124, 132
Gobbi, Tito, b 38, 92, *94*, 102, *123*, *124*, *127*, *128*, *129*, *130*, *133*, *150*, 155*, 168
Godfrey, Isadore, c *114*, 115, 116, 117
Goldberg, Reiner, t 20, 139
González, Dalmacio, t 50
Gorr, Rita, ms 106, *107*
Grace, Nicholas, b 115
Gramatzki, Ilse, ms 111
Gray, Fenton, b 117
Green, Adolph, b 24
Greindl, Josef, ba 41, 138
Grist, Reri, s 77, 121
Groves, Charles, c 116, 117
Gruberová, Edita, s 38, 54, 109, 129, 131, *132*, 167

Index of Artists

Grümmer, Elisabeth, s 54, 135, 140
Grundheber, Franz, b 54
Gueden, Hilde, s 85, 167
Gui, Vittorio, c 104
Guittard, Lawrence, b 98
Gunn, Rosemary, ms 52

Hadley, Jerry, t 24, 47, 57, 68, 102
Hagegård, Håkan, b *102*
Hagley, Alison, s 78
Haitink, Bernhard, c *20*, 112, 139, *140*
Halász, Michael, c 79
Hale, Robert, b 134
Halgrimson, Amanda, s 75, *76*
Hall, Juanita, ms 100
Hallstein, Ingeborg, s 20
Hamari, Julia, ms 111
Hampson, Thomas, b 47, 74, 84, *85*, 102, 118
Hanley, Regina, s 115, 116
Harnoncourt, Nikolaus, c 77, *111*
Harrhy, Eiddwen, s 51
Harrison, Rex, b *68*
Harwood, Elizabeth, s 61, 85, 116, 117
Haskins, Virginia, s 98
Hauptmann, Cornelius, ba 77
Haymon, Cynthia, s 43
Heger, Robert, c 41
Heilmann, Uwe, t 167
Henderson, Skitch, c 43
Hendricks, Barbara, s 28, 35, 43, 46, 54, 95, 112, 124
Heppner, Ben, t *136*, 168
Hickox, Richard, c *51*, 52
Hiestermann, Horst, t 113
Hill Smith, Marilyn, s 56, 101, 117
Hofmann, Peter, t *65*, 134
Holland, Lyndsie, ms 116
Holloway, Stanley, b 68
Hollweg, Werner, t 61
Holm, Renate, s 59, 72
Hopf, Hans, t *136*

Horne, Marilyn, ms 21, 26, *51*, 63, 83, *94*, 96, *97*, *105*, 156*, 167
Hornik, Gottfried b 79
Hotter, Hans, b 139
Howard, Jason, b 57
Hubbard, Bruce, ba 57
Humburg, Will, c 102

Ilosvay, Maria von, s 54
Inghilleri, Giovanni, b 85
Irons, Jeremy, b 68

Jacobs, René, c 52
Janowitz, Gundula, s 140
Janowski, Masrek, c 140
Jerusalem, Siegfried, t 41, 59, *60*, *111*, 135, *138*
Jo, Sumi, s 79, 121, 167
Jobin, Raoul, t 49
Jochum, Eugen, c *136*
Johnson, Van, b 67
Jones, Della, ms 51, 52, 53
Jones, Gareth, b 117
Jones, Gwyneth, s 54
Jones, Shirley, s 98
Jungwirth, Manfred, ba 112

Kaludov, Kaludi, t 90, 168
Karajan, Herbert von, c *20*, 27, 54, *55*, 61, 63, *64*, *70*, 74, 75, 79, 80, 85, 88, *89*, 92, *109*, 112, *113*, 120, 121, 122, *124*, *134*, *136*, 138, *139*
Kavrakos, Dimitri, ba 21
Kaye, Judy, ms 67
Keilberth, Joseph, c 140
Kéléman, Zoltán, ba 20
Kelly, Gene, b *67*
Kelly, Janice, s 57
Kempe, Rudolf, c 108, 135
Kenny, Yvonne, s 52, 77
Kerns, Robert, b 88
King, James, t 132
Kingsley, Ben, b 96, *97*
Kirk, Lisa, ms 84

Index of Artists

Kleiber, Carlos, c 131, 140
Kleiber, Erich, c *113*
Klemperer, Otto, c 20
Knight, Gillian, ms 117
Kohn, Christian, ba 140
Kollo, René, t *58*, 61, *108*, 136, 137, *138*
Kopp, Miroslav, t 108
Kostal, Irwin, c 99
Kotcherga, Anatoly, ba 80
Kraus, Alfredo, t 22, *49*, 70, 71, *132*, 168
Krause, Tom, b 167
Krombholc, Jaroslav, c 108
Kubiak, Teresa, s 118
Kuhlmann, Kathleen, ms 51
Kunz, Erich, b 59, 61, 109, *111*
Kusche, Benno, ba 111
Kwella, Patrizia, s 51
Kwon, Hellen, s 79

La Scola, Vincenzo, t 21
Lagger, Peter, ba 136
Lakes, Gary, t *140*
Lane, Nathan, b 43, 66
Langston, John, b 24
Lanza, Mario, t *101*, 168
Larmore, Jennifer, ms *52*, 54, *102*, 104, 105
Lazzari, Agostino, t 94
Lazzarini, Adriana, ms 129
Lear, Evelyn, s 168
Lee, Bill, t 100
Leech, Richard, t 47, 109
Legay, Henri, t 70
Leiferkus, Sergei, b 80, 128
Leinsdorf, Erich, c 58, 94, 121
Leppard, Raymond, c *46*
Levine, James, c 33, 36, 44, 69, 74, 90, 118, 125, 132, *140*
Lewis, Richard, t *115*
Licette, Miriam, s *48*
Ligabue, Ilva, s 124
Ligendza, Catarina, s 136

Lind, Eva, s 54, 82, 109
Lindner, Brigitte, s 59, 111
Lipovšek, Marjana, ms 54, 80
Lippert, Herbert, t 79, 111
Lloyd, Robert, ba 53, 126
Lombard, Alain, c 34
Loose, Emmy, s 59, 61
Lopardo, Frank, t 35, *36*, *102*, 105
Lorengar, Pilar, s *108*, 167
Ludwig, Christa, ms 20, 24, 88, 112, 121, 135, 137, 138, 167
Luker, Rebecca, s 67
Luxon, Benjamin, b 58

Maazel, Lorin, c 43, 91, 94, 128
Mackerras, Charles, c 52, *74*, 115, 116, 117, 118
MacNeil, Cornell, b 87, 120
MacRae, Gordon, b 98
Malas, Spiro, b 36, 37
Malfitano, Catherine, s 49
Manuel, Paul, t 26
Manuguerra, Matteo, b 22, 71, 131
Margiono, Charlotte, s 75
Marin, Ion, c 38, 105
Marriner, Neville, c 74, 79, 104, 117
Martin, Mary, s 99, *100*
Martinelli, Giovanni, t *148*
Martinpelto, Hillevi, s 78
Martinucci, Nicola, t 63, *64*
Marton, Eva, s 29, 32, 87, 139, 168
Mas, Margaret, s 94
Maslennikov, Alexei, t 80
Masterson, Valerie, s 52, 116
Matacic, Lovro von, c 61
Mathis, Edith, s 79, 140
Mattes, Willy, c 56, 59
Matteuzzi, William, t 102
Mattila, Karita, s 74
Mauceri, John, c 24, 68, 96
McArthur, Edwin, c 57
McCormack, John, t 146
McGlinn, John, c 57, 67, 84
McKay, Margery, ms 99

McLaughlin, Marie, s 116
Mehta, Zubin, c 87, 95, 132
Mei, Eva, s 21, 35
Meier, Waltraut, ms 106, *107*, 135, *138*
Melba, Nellie, s *24, 49, 143, 144*, 145, 145*
Mentzer, Susanne, ms 102
Merrill, Robert, b *28, 39*, 83, 85, 94, 121, 168
Merriman, Nan, ms 74, 124
Mesplé, Mady, s 34, *35*, 71
Metternich, Josef, b 54
Micheau, Janine, s 27, 49
Milanov, Zinka, s 120, 132, *133*
Millet, Danielle, ms 34
Millo, Aprile, s *120*, 132, *133*
Mills, Erie, s 24
Milnes, Sherrill, b 27, 33, 38, 44, 63, 83, 87, 92, 94, 122, 125, 126, 129, 131, 132, 167
Minton, Yvonne, ms 78, 112, *113*
Mitchell, Leona, s 43
Mitchell, Warren, b 68
Moffo, Anna, s 78, *91*, 168
Molinari-Pradelli, Francesco, c 91, 95
Moll, Kurt, ba 77, *112*, 134, 135, 136, *140*, 167
Mollet, Pierre, b 49
Monteux, Pierre, c 70, 71
Monti, Nicola, t 23
Morison, Elsie, s *115*
Morison, Patricia, s 84, *85*
Morris, James, b *76*, 113, 132, 139, *140*
Moser, Edda, s 56
Moyle, Julian, b 116
Murray, Ann, ms 54, 74, 82
Muti, Riccardo, c 21, 22, 35, 120, 123, 125, 126

Nash, Heddle, t *48*
Nash, Royston, c 116
Neblett, Carol, s *58, 87*

Nelson, John, c 53
Nelsson, Wlodomar, c 134
Nesterenko, Yevgeny, ba 127
Neukirch, Harald, t 77
Neumann, Václav, c 40
Neway, Patricia, s *99*
Newman, Alfred, c 96, 100
Nilsson, Birgit, s 95, *96, 114*, 138, *139*, 156*
Nimsgern, Siegmund, b 135
Nixon, Marni, s 26, 68, 96, *97*
Norberg-Schulz, Elisabeth, s 79
Norman, Jessye, s *20*, 78, 82, *113, 135, 140*, 157*, 168
Norrington, Roger, c 75
Novák, Richard, ba 40, 108
Nucci, Leo, b 33, 35, 36, 44, 91, 102, 121, 122, 124, 128, 130, 167

O'Neill, Dennis, t 87
Obraztsova, Elena, ms 33
Ochman, Wieslaw, t 40
Oestman, Arnold, c 79
Oke, Alan, b 115
Olafimihan, Tinuke, s 26
Ollmann, Kurt, b 26
Olsen, Stanford, t 77
Oncina, Juán, t 104
Organosova, Luba, s 75, 77
Ornadel, Cyril, c 68
Ott, Karin, s 79
Ozawa, Seiji, c *113*

Panerai, Rolando, b 22, 69, 74, 85, 88, 94, 124
Patané, Giuseppe, c 29, 63, 94, 102
Patinkin, Mandy, t 100
Pavarotti, Luciano, t *8, 22*, 23, 29, 36, *37*, 38, *39, 41*, 44, *45*, 63, 64, 83, 85, *86*, 88, *89, 90, 92, 93*, 95, *96*, 121, *128*, 129, 131, *133, 151*, 154, 158*, 167, 168
Perlea, Jonel, c 120
Pert, Jill, ms 117

Index of Artists

Petina, Irra, ms 24
Phipps, Simon, c 115, 117
Pinza. Ezio, ba *100*, 159
Pirazzini, Miriam, ms 88
Plasson, Michel, c 28, 47, 49, 70, 71
Plishka, Paul, ba 125
Plowright, Rosalind, s 82, 125, 132
Plummer, Christopher, b 99
Pons, Juán, b 38
Pons, Lily, a *37*
Popp, Lucia, s 41, 58, 78, 109, 167
Potter, Philip, t 117
Prandelli, Giacinto, t 85, 94
Praticó, Bruno, b 36
Prêtre, Georges, c 28, 47, 71, 106, *107*
Prevedi, Bruno, t 127
Previn, André, c 68, *109*
Prey, Hermann, b 41, *58*, 72, 73, *111*, 140, 167
Price, Leontyne, s *43*, 92, *93*, 94, 121, 122, 123, 125, 132, 158*, 167, 168
Price, Margaret, s 121, 122, 168
Prince, Faith, ms 66
Pritchard, John, c 36
Protschka, Josef, t 111, 134
Protti, Aldo, b 162
Pryce-Jones, John, c 115, 116, 117
Pushee, Graham, ct 52

Quilico, Gino, b 28, 35, 49, 70, 104, 167
Quivar, Florence, ms 121

Raffeiner, Walter, t 113
Ragin, Derek Lee, ct 52
Rahbari, Alexander, c 63, 90
Raimondi, Ruggero, ba 92, *102*, 104, 122, 125, 126
Ramey, Samuel, ba *22*, 29, 38, 47, 53, 75, 78, 79, 80, 82, 92, *93*, *102*, *105*, 159*, 167
Randová, Eva, ms 135

Rattle, Simon, c 43
Read, Michael, c 64
Reed, John, b *114*, 117
Rees, Deborah, s 116
Rehfuss, Heinz, b 49
Remedios, Ramón, t 56
Rendall, David, t 91, 101
Rescigno, Nicola, c 92
Resnik, Regina, ms 124
Ricciarelli, Katia, s 27, 92, *93*, 95, *96*, *120*, 122, 124, 128, *130*
Richard, Lawrence, b 59
Ridderbusch, Karl, ba 20, 41, 136, 138
Ritchie, Elizabeth, s 115
Rizzi, Carlo, c 47, 104, 131
Roberts, Eric, b 116, 117
Roebuck, Janine, ms 115
Röhrholm, Marianne, ms 52
Rolfe-Johnson, Anthony, t 53, 116
Rosenshein, Neil, t 118
Ross, Lesley Echo, s 115, 117
Rossi-Lemeni, Nicola, ba 21, 22
Rothenberger, Anneliese, s 41, 56, 59, *60*, 73
Rouleau, Joseph, ba 105
Rounseville, Robert, t 24
Ruffo, Titta, b 145
Runnicles, Donald, c 54
Ruziczka, Else, ms 41
Rydl, Kurt, ba 79, 112, 134, 140
Rysanek, Lotte, s 113, *128*, 139

Salminen, Matti, ba 77, 134, *138*
Sandford, Kenneth, b 117
Sandison, Gordon, b 115, 117
Santi, Nello, c 63
Santini, Gabriele, c 88, 94, 130
Sarabria, Guillermo, b 28
Sardinero, Vicente, b 90
Sargent, Malcolm, c *115*, 116, 117
Sawallisch, Wolfgang, c *136*, 137
Schade, Michael, t 115
Schädle, Lotte, s 111

Index of Artists

Schasching, Rudolf, b 111
Schippers, Thomas, c 123
Schlick, Barbara, s 52
Schmidt, Andreas, b 54, 75, 137, 140
Schreier, Peter, t 77, 140
Schüler, Johannes, c 41
Schumann-Heink, Ernestine, ms 145
Schunk, Robert, t 134
Schwarz, Hanna, s 54
Schwarzkopf, Elisabeth, s 54, *55*, 59, *60*, *61*, *74*, 75, *76*, 78, *79*, *109*, 111, *112*, *113*, 124, *136*, *139*, *155*, 159*
Sciutti, Graziella, s 51, 168
Scotto, Renata, s *33*, 44, *45*, 69, 88, *89*, *94*, 95,
Scovotti, Jeannette, s 96
Seiffert, Peter, t 94, 109, 140
Serafin, Tullio, c 21, 22, 29, 38, 69, 85, 94, 128, 129
Sereni, Mario, b 88, 91, 123
Serge, John, t 105
Serra, Luciana, s 82
Servile, Robert, b 102, 168
Shicoff, Neil, t 38, 82, 118, 129, 131
Shilling, Eric, b 116
Shirley, Bill, t 68
Sieden, Cyndia, s 77
Siepi, Cesare, ba 29, *39*
Sigmundsson, Kristin, ba 79
Silja, Anja, s 137
Simionato, Giulietta, ms 33, 94, 120
Simoneau, Leopold, t 28, 74
Sinclair, Monico, ms 51
Sinopoli, Giuseppe, c 90, 92, *113*, 125, *126*, 127, 129, 137, *138*
Skovhus, Boje, b 61
Slatkin, Leonard, c 87
Smith, Muriel, ms 100
Söderstrom, Elisabeth, s 167
Soffel, Doris, ms 41
Solti, Georg, c 27, 78, 112, *113*, *114*, 118, 121, *124*, 128, 130, *135*, 137, *138*, 139
Sotin, Hans, ba 135

Soukopová, Vera, ms 40
Soyer, Roger, b 34, 71
Spagnoli, Pietro, b 36
Speiser, Elisabeth, s 46
Spencer, Kenneth, ba 57
Spiess, Ludovic, t 80
Steffek, Hanny, s 61
Steinberg, Pinchas, c 32
Stella, Antonietta, s 168
Stephen, Pamela Helen, ms 78
Stich-Randall, Teresa, s 112
Stiedry, Fritz, c 46
Stignani, Ebe, ms 21
Stolz, Robert, c 111
Stratas, Teresa, s *57*, 61, *108*
Strauss, Edward, c 66
Streich, Rita, s 72
Streit, Kurt, t 79, 117,
Studer, Cheryl, s 38, *39*, 47, *48*, 61, 79, 82, *105*, *113*, *128*, 135, *136*, 137, *138*, 139 160*
Suart, Richard, b 115, 116, 117
Suliotis, Elena, s *127*
Sullivan, Lee, b 67
Summers, Jonathan, b 106
Suthaus, Ludwig, t 138
Sutherland, Joan, s *21*, *22*, *23*, *24*, *33*, *34*, 35, 36, *37*, 38, *39*, 47, *51*, *61*, 75, *76*, *82*, 95, *96*, *105*, 131, *132*, *133*, *160*, 161*, 167
Sweet, Sharon, s *140*

Tabbert, William, t 100
Taddei, Giuseppe, b 63, 75, 78, 92, *93*
Talvela, Martti, ba 80, 138, 167
Tappy, Eric, t 168
Tate, Jeffrey, c 54, 82
Te Kanawa, Kiri, s 26, 27, *68*, 74, 78, 79, *91*, *100*, 109, *112*, *113*, 118, *128*, *130*, 162*, 167
Tebaldi, Renata, s 21, 29, *30*, 32, *33*, 44, *45*, 69, 83, *84*, 85, *86*, *87*, 94, 120, *154*, 161*, 167

177

Index of Artists

Terfel, Bryn, b 78, 113, 117
Thebom, Blanche, ms 138
Thomas, Davis, ba 53
Thomas, Jess, t 134, *135*
Tichy, Georg, t 79, 168
Tierney, Vivien, s 59, 122
Titus, Alan, b 32
Tomlinson, John, ba 51, 52
Tomova-Sintow, Anna, s 75, *112*
Tourangeau, Huguette, ms 82, 129
Tozzi, Giorgio, ba *100*
Trost, Rainer, t 61
Troyanos, Tatiana, ms 26, 27, 71
Tucci, Gabriela, s 168
Tucker, Richard, t *41*, 167, 168
Tumagian, Eduard, ba 63

Upshaw, Dawn, s 168
Uzounov, Dimiter, t 168

Valentini, Lucia, ms 122, 124
Van Allan, ba 117
Van Dam, José, b 27, 47, *48*, 49, 79, 82, 113, 134
Vanzo, Alain, t 28, *34*
Varady, Julia, s 50, 167, 168
Vargas, Ramón, t 102
Vejzovic, Dunja, ms *134*
Verrett, Shirley, ms 121, 122, *126*
Vickers, Jon, t *20*, 106, *107*, *128*, 138, *139*, 157
Vinco, Ivo, ba 83
Viotti, Marcello, c 36
Vishnevskaya, Galina, s 80
Vlachopoulos, Zoë, s 46
Von Otter, Sophie, s 54, 74, 82, 112

Von Stade, Frederica, ms 57, 71, *72*, 78
Votto, Antonino, c 23, 83

Waechter, Eberhard, b 61, 75, 78, 137, 138, 168
Wand, Betty, ms 26
Warfield, William, ba *43*
Warnford, Nicholas, b 26
Warren, Leonard, b 120, 132
Weikl, Bernd, b 54, 118, 136, 140, 167
Weir, Leonard, t 68
Welker, Hartmut, b 135
Wewel, Günter, ba 73
White, Willard, ba 43, 57
Wildhaber, Helmut, t 80
Winbergh, Gösta, t 35, 75
Windgassen, Wolfgang, t 137, 138, *139*, 157
Witt, Kerstin, ms 113
Wixell, Ingvar, b 36, 63, 78, 94
Wlaschiha, Ekkehard, b 20
Woollett, Elizabeth, s 116
Wordsworth, Barry, c 56, 59
Wright, Colin, t 116
Wunderlich, Fritz, t 108

Yurisich, Gregory, b 75

Zaccaria, Nicola, ba 23
Zajick, Dolores, ms 132
Zampieri, Mara, s 126
Zanasi, Furio, ba 52
Zancanaro, Giorgio, b 125, 131, 132
Zareska, Eugenia, s 80

Index of most popular arias, duets, etc.

Page numbers in *italics* indicate additional textual inclusion.

A te, o cara *I puritani* 22
Ach, so fromm *Martha* 41
Addio a la madre *Cavalleria rusticana* 69
Ah, fors é lui, *La traviata* 131
Ah, non credea mirarti *La sonnambula* 23
Ai nostri monti *Il trovatore* 132
Air des bijoux *Faust* 47
All I ask of you *Phantom of the Opera* 65
Als flotter Geist *Der Zigeunerbaron* 111
Ardon gl'incensi *Lucia di Lammermoor* 38
Au fond du temple *The Pearl Fishers* 28
Avant de quitter *Faust* 47
Barcarolle *Tales of Hoffmann* 82
Bell Song *Lakmé* 34
Bella figlia dell'amore *Rigoletto* 129
Bess, you is my woman now *Porgy and Bess* 43
Calf of Gold *Faust* 47
Can't help lovin' dat man *Show Boat* 57
Caro nome *Rigoletto* 129
Casta diva *Norma* 21
Catalogue Aria *Don Giovanni* 75
Celeste Aida *Aida* 120
Ch'ella mi creda libero *Girl of the Golden West* 87
Che farò senza Euridice *Orfeo ed Euridice* 46
Che gelida manina *La bohème* 85
Chi mi frena *Lucia di Lammermoor* 38
Cielo e mar *La gioconda* 83
Climb every mountain *The Sound of Music* 99
Come un bel dì di maggio *Andrea Chénier* 44
Dalla sua pace *Don Giovanni* 75
Dance Duet *Hänsel and Gretel* 54
Deep in my heart *The Student Prince* 101
Der Hölle Rache *Magic Flute* 79
Di provenza il mar *La traviata* 131
Di quella pira *Il trovatore* 132
Doll Song *Tales of Hoffmann* 82
Donna non vidi mai *Manon Lescaut* 90
Dove sono *Marriage of Figaro* 78
Down her cheek a pearly tear, *see* Una furtiva lagrima
Dream, The *Manon* 70
Drinking Song *La traviata* 131
Drinking Song *The Student Prince* 101
E lucevan le stelle *Tosca* 92
Easter Hymn *Cavalleria rusticana* 69
Ebben, ne andrò lontana *La Wally* 32
Ecco ridente *The Barber of Seville* 102
Edelweiss *The Sound of Music* 99
Eri tu *Un ballo in maschera* 121
Even bravest hearts *Faust* 47
Flower Duet *Lakmé*, *see* Viens, Mallika
Flower Duet *Madama Butterfly* 88
Flower Song *Carmen* 27

Index of most popular arias, duets, etc.

Glitter and be gay *Candide* 24
Glück, das mir verblieb *Die tote Stadt* 58
Habanera *Carmen* 27
Home to our mountains, *see* 'Ai nostri monti'
I could have danced all night *My Fair Lady* 68
I feel pretty *West Side Story* 26
Iago's Creed *Otello* 128
Il mio tesoro *Don Giovanni* 75
Improvviso *Andrea Chénier* 44
In quelle trine morbide *Manon Lescaut* 90
In the depth of the temple *The Pearl Fishers* 28
It must be so *Candide* 24
Je crois entendre *The Pearl Fishers* 28
Jewel Song *Faust* 47
La ci darem la mano *Don Giovanni* 75
La donna é mobile *Rigoletto* 129
La mamma morta *Andrea Chénier* 44
Largo al factotum *The Barber of Seville* 102
Last rose of summer *Martha* 41
Laughing Song *Die Fledermaus* 109
Le veau d'or *Faust* 47
Lenski's Aria *Eugene Onegin* 118
Libiamo! *La traviata* 131
Liebestod *Tristan und Isolde* 138
Lippen schweigen *The Merry Widow* 61
Love and music, *see* Vissi d'arte
Love Duet *Madama Butterfly* 88
Lovely maid in the moonlight, *see* O soave fanciulla
M'appari *Martha* 41
Mad Scene *Lucia di Lammermoor* 38
Make believe *Show Boat* 57
Maria *West Side Story* 26
Martern aller Arten *Abduction from the Seraglio* 77
Mein Herr Marquis *Die Fledermaus* 109
Merry Widow Waltz 61
Mira, o Norma *Norma* 21
Miserere *Il trovatore* 132
Mon coeur s'ouvre *Samson and Delilah* 106
Musetta's Waltz Song *La bohème* 85
Music of the Night *Phantom of the Opera* 65
Nemico della patria *Andrea Chénier* 44
Nessun dorma *Turandot* 95
Non più andrai *Marriage of Figaro* 78
None shall sleep *Turandot* 95
O don fatale *Don Carlos* 122
O du mein holder Abendstern *Tannhäuser* 137
O mio babbino caro *Gianni Schicchi* 94
O silver moon *Rusalka* 40
O sleep, why dost thou leave me *Semele* 53
O soave fanciulla *La bohème* 85
O Star of Eve *Tannhäuser* 137
Oh, my beloved daddy *Gianni Schicchi* 94
Oh, what a beautiful morning *Oklahoma!* 98
Ol' man river *Show Boat* 57
On the street where you live *My Fair Lady* 68
On with the motley *Pagliacci* 63
One fine day *Madama Butterfly* 88
Open Road *The Gypsy Baron* 111
Play, Gypsy *Gräfin Mariza* 56
Porgi amor *Marriage of Figaro* 78
Pour mon âme *La Fille du régiment* 37, *38*
Pourquoi me reveiller *Werther* 71
Prayer *Hänsel and Gretel* 54
Prendi, l'anel ti dono *La sonnambula* 23
Prisoners' Chorus *Nabucco*, *see* Va pensiero
Prize Song *Mastersingers of Nuremberg* 136

Index of most popular arias, duets, etc.

Prologue *Pagliacci* 63
Quartet, Bella figlia dell'amore *Rigoletto* 129
Queen of the Night's Aria *Magic Flute, see* Der Hölle Rache
Questa o quella *Rigoletto* 129
Qui la voce *I puritani* 22
Rachel, quand du Seigneur *La Juive* 50
Recondita armonia *Tosca* 92
Ride of the Valkyries *Die Walküre* 139
Salut! demeure *Faust* 47
Seguidilla *Carmen* 27
Sempre libera *La traviata, see* Ah, fors è lui
Senza mamma *Suor Angelica* 93
Sextet, Chi mi frena *Lucia di Lammermoor* 38
Si, mi chiamano Mimì *La bohème* 85
Softly awakes my heart *Samson and Delilah* 106
Soldier's Chorus *Faust* 47
Solenne in quest'ora *La forza del destino* 125
Some enchanted evening *South Pacific* 100
Somewhere *West Side Story* 26
Spargi d'amaro *Lucia di Lammermoor* 38
Strange harmony of contrasts, *see* Recondita armonia
Suicidio *La gioconda* 83
Summertime *Porgy and Bess* 44
Suoni la tromba *I puritani* 22
The stars were brightly shining, *see* E lucevan le stelle
They call me Mimì, *see* Si, mi chiamano Mimì
Tonight *West Side Story* 26
Toreador Song *Carmen* 27
Tornami a dir *Don Pasquale* 35
Triumphal March *Aida* 120
Un bel di *Madama Butterfly* 88
Un di all'azzurro *Andrea Chénier, see* Improvviso
Una furtiva lagrima *L'elisir d'amore* 37
Una voce poco fa *The Barber of Seville* 102
Va pensiero *Nabucco* 127
Vesti la giubba *Pagliacci* 63
Viens, Mallika *Lakmé* 34
Vilja *The Merry Widow* 61
Vissi d'arte *Tosca* 92
Voi che sapete *Marriage of Figaro* 78
Voi lo sapete, mamma *Cavalleria rusticana* 69
Waltz Song *Roméo et Juliette* 49
Wedding March *Lohengrin* 135
Where'er you walk *Semele* 53
Willow Song *Otello* 128
Wunderbar *Kiss Me, Kate* 84
You are my heart's delight *Land of Smiles* 60
Your tiny hand is frozen, *see* Che gelida manina

Index of Operas

Page numbers in *italics* indicate major entries.

Abduction from the Seraglio, The (Mozart) *27*, 167
Adriana Lecouvreur (Cilea) *33*, 148, 149, 150, 152, 155, 162
Africana, L' (Meyerbeer) 144, 148, 149, 152,
Aida (Verdi) 120, 144, 145, 148, 149, 151, 152, 154, 158, 159, 162, 168
Alceste (Gluck) 156
Alcina (Handel) *51*
Allegro, il penseroso, L' (Handel) 146
Amico Fritz, L' (Mascagni) 152
Andrea Chénier (Giordano) *44*, 148, 150, 152, 153, 154, 156, 162, 168
Anna Bolena (Donizetti) 150
Arabella (R Strauss)
Ariadne auf Naxos (R Strauss) 160
Arlesiana, L' (Cilea) 33, 149, 153, 156, 167
Attila (Verdi) 161
Ballo in maschera, Un (Verdi) *121*, 144, 145, 148, 149, 152, 154, 156, 159
Barber of Seville, The (Rossini) *102*, see also *Barbiere di Siviglia*
Barbiere di Siviglia, Il (Rossini) 35, *102*, 104, 150, 156, 161, 167, 168
Bartered Bride, The (Smetana) *108*
Beggar Student, The (Millöcker) *72*
Belle Hélène, La (Offenbach) 157
Bettelstudent, Der (Millöcker) *72*
Bianca e Farnando (Bellini) 155

Boccaccio (Suppé) 160
Bohème, La (Leoncavallo) 145, 152
Bohème, La (Puccini) *85*, 87, 145, 146, 148, 149, 151, 152, 153, 154, 155, 158, 159, 162, 163, 167, 168
Boris Godounov (Mussorgsky) *80*, 168
Brigadoon (Loewe) *67*
Caïd, Le (Thomas) 159
Candide (Bernstein) *24*, 155
Capriccio (R Strauss) 10, 160
Capuleti e i Montechi, Le (Bellini) 156
Carmen (Bizet) 14, *27*, 86, 149, 152, 153, 154, 155, 156, 158, 159, 168
Cavalleria rusticana (Mascagni) 32, 63, *69*, 149, 151, 152, 153, 154, 167
Cenerentola, La (Rossini) *104*, 147, 153, 156, 159, 167
Chérubin (Massenet)
Cinderella (Rossini) *104*, see also *Cenerentola*
Clemenza di Tito (Mozart) 156
Contes d'Hoffmann, Les (Offenbach) *82*, 154, 159, 161, 168
Così fan tutte (Mozart) *74*, 168
Count of Luxemburg, The (Lehár) *59*, 160
Countess Maritza (Kálmán) *56*
Csárdásfürstin, Die (Kálmán) *56*
Daughter of the Regiment, The (Donizetti) *37*, see also *Fille du régiment*
Dead City, The (Korngold) *58*
Dinorah (Meyerbeer) 150

Index of Operas

Don Carlos (Verdi) *122*, 130, 148, 151, 156, 163
Don César de Bazan (Massenet) 145
Don Giovanni (Mozart) 74, 75, 147, 156, 160, 161, 167, 168
Don Pasquale (Donizetti) *35*, 36
Don Quichotte (Massenet) 159
Don Sebastiano (Donizetti) 144
Donna del lago, La (Rossini) 147, 156
Dubarry, Die (Millöcker)
Duca d'Alba, Il (Donizetti) 144
Edgar (Puccini) 159
Elektra (R Strauss) 161
Elisir d'amore, L' (Donizetti) *36*, 144, 149, 150, 151, 153, 154, 156, 168
Entführung aus dem Serail, Die (Mozart) 77, 167
Ernani (Verdi) *123*, 152, 153, 159, 161
Eugene Onegin (Tchaikovsky) *118*, 154
Euryanthe (Weber) 157
Evita (Lloyd Webber) 65
Falstaff (Verdi) 30, *124*, 155
Fanciulla del West, La (Puccini) *87*, 149, 152, 153, 156, 159, 162
Faust (Gounod) 30, *47*, 145, 149, 153, 158, 159, 161, 162
Fedora (Giordano) 149, 152
Fidelio (Beethoven) *20*
Fille du régiment, La (Donizetti) *37*, 150
Fledermaus, Die (J Strauss) 61, *109*, 160
Fliegende Holländer, Der (Wagner) *134*, 157
Flying Dutchman, The (Wagner) *134*, 157
Force of Destiny, The (Verdi) *125*, see also *Forza del destino*
Forza del destino, La (Verdi) *125*, 144, 145, 148, 152, 153, 154, 156, 159, 162, 168
Frau ohne Schatten, Die (R Strauss) 161
Freischütz, Der (Weber) *140*

Gasparone (Millöcker) 73
Gianni Schicchi (Puccini) *93*, 149, 153, 155, 159, 162, 163, 167, 168
Gioconda, La (Ponchielli) *83*, 148, 149, 152, 153, 168
Girl of the Golden West, The (Puccini) see *Fanciulla del West*
Gisélidis (Massenet) 159
Giuditta (Lehár) 160
Giulio Cesare (Handel) 51, *52*
Gondoliers, The (Sullivan) *115*
Götterdämmerung, Die (Wagner) 157
Graf von Luxemburg, Der (Lehár) *59*, 160
Gräfin Mariza (Kálmán) *56*
Guys and Dolls (Loesser) *66*
Gypsy Baron, The (J Strauss) *111*
Gypsy Princess, The (Kálmán) *56*
Hänsel und Gretel (Humperdinck) *54*
HMS Pinafore (Sullivan) *115*
Huguenots, Les (Meyerbeer) 159
Iolanthe (Sullivan) *116*
Italiana in Algeri, L' (Rossini) 147, 156, 159
Jolie fille de Perth, La (Bizet) 159
Jongleur de Notre Dame, Le (Massenet) 159
Juive, La (Halévy) *50*, 144
Julius Caesar (Handel) 51, *53*
King and I, The (Rodgers) 68, *96*
Kiss Me, Kate (Porter) 68, *96*
Lakmé (Délibes) *34*, 150, 161, 167
Land des Lächelns, Das (Lehár) *60*
Land of Smiles, The (Lehár) *60*
Linda di Chamounix (Donizetti) 161
Lohengrin (Wagner) *135*, 146, 152, 153, 154, 157
Lucia di Lammermoor (Donizetti) 22, *38*, 146, 151, 156, 160, 161, 167
Lucrezia Borgia (Donizetti) 161
Luisa Miller (Verdi) 148, 151, 154
Lustige Witwe, Die (Lehár) *61*, 160
Macbeth (Verdi) *126*, 127, 156, 159, 167

Index of Operas

Madama Butterfly (Puccini) 87, *88*, 152, 155, 159, 162, 163, 167, 168

Magic Flute, The (Mozart) 79, see also *Zauberflöte*

Manon (Massenet) *70*, 90, 144, 149, 153, 155

Manon Lescaut (Puccini) 70, *90*, 144, 148, 151, 152, 155, 159, 162, 163, 167, 168

Marriage of Figaro, The (Mozart) 78, see also *Nozze di Figaro*

Martha (Flotow) *41*, 149, 154, 158, 168

Masked Ball, A (Verdi) 121, see also *Ballo in maschera*

Mastersingers of Nuremberg, The (Wagner) *136*, 161

Mefistofole (Boito) *29*, 150, 153, 155, 162

Meistersinger von Nürnberg, Die (Wagner) *136*, 161

Merry Widow, The (Lehár) 56, *61*

Mikado, The (Sullivan) *116*

My Fair Lady (Loewe) *68*

Nabucco (Verdi) *127*, 156

Norma (Bellini) *21*, 149, 154, 157, 161, 167

Nozze di Figaro, Le (Mozart) 74, 78, 146, 147, 153, 155, 156, 160, 167, 168

Obersteiger, Der (Zeller) 160

Oklahoma! (Rodgers) 84, *98*

Opera Ball, The (Heuberger) 160

Orfeo ed Euridice (Gluck) *46*, 168

Orpheus and Euridice (Gluck) 46

Otello (Rossini) 147

Otello (Verdi) 30, *128*, 145, 146, 147, 152, 153, 154, 156, 159, 162, 167

Pagliacci (Leoncavallo) 32, *63*, 69, 93, 144, 145, 149, 151, 152, 155, 156, 158, 162, 168

Patience (Sullivan) *116*

Pearl Fishers, The (Bizet) *28*, see also *Pêcheurs de perles*

Pêcheurs de perles, Les (Bizet) *28*, 153, 155, 167, 168

Périchole, La (Offenbach) 151

Phantom of the Opera, The (Lloyd Webber) *64*

Pietra del paragone, La (Rossini) 147

Pirata, Il (Bellini) 150

Pirates of Penzance, The (Sullivan) *117*

Porgy and Bess (Gershwin) *43*

Puritani, I (Bellini) *22*, 124, 155, 158, 159, 161

Queen of Spades (Tchaikovsky) 168

Re pastore, Il (Mozart) 145, 167

Regina di Saba, La (Goldmark) 144

Rheingold, Das (Wagner) 139

Rigoletto (Verdi) 10, 15, *129*, 144, 145, 146, 149, 154, 156, 158, 167, 168

Ring des Nibelungen, Der (Wagner) *137*, 139

Rodelinda (Handel) 156

Roi dys, Le (Lalo) 145, 146

Romeo and Juliet (Gounod) *49*, see also *Roméo et Juliette*

Roméo et Juliette (Gounod) *49*, 157, 168

Rondine, La (Puccini) *91*, 155, 159, 163, 167

Rosamunda d'Inghilterra (Donizetti) 161

Rosenkavalier, Der (R Strauss) *112*, 159, 160, 167

Ruddigore (Sullivan) *117*

Rusalka (Dvořák) *40*

Salome (R Strauss) 105, *113*, 160

Samson (Handel) 163

Samson and Delilah (Saint-Saëns) *106*, 149, 156

Sapho (Gounod) 156

Schiavo, Lo (Gomes) 144

Semele (Handel) *53*, 156

Semiramide (Rossini) *105*, 156, 159, 161, 167

Seraglio, The, see *Entführung aus dem Serail*

Show Boat (Kern) 57, 185
Siège de Corinthe, La (Rossini) 159
Simon Boccanegra (Verdi) *130*
Sonnambula, La (Bellini) *23*, 161
Sound of Music, The (Rodgers) *99*
South Pacific (Rodgers) *100*
Student Prince, The (Romberg) *101*
Suor Angelica (Puccini) *93*, 155, 162
Tabarro, Il (Puccini) *93*
Tales of Hoffmann, The (Offenbach) *82*, see also *Contes d'Hoffmann*
Tancredi (Rossini) 147
Tannhäuser (Wagner) *137*, 153, 157
Tosca (Puccini) 8, 45, *92*, 98, 144, 145, 146, 148, 149, 150, 151, 152, 153, 154, 155, 157, 158, 159, 168
Tote Stadt, Die (Korngold) *58*
Traviata, La (Verdi) 8, 131, 145, 146, 149, 153, 154, 155, 156, 159, 161, 162, 163, 167, 168
Tristan und Isolde (Wagner) *138*, 157, 161, 168
Trittico, Il (Puccini) *93*
Trovatore, Il (Verdi) *132*, 144, 145, 148, 149, 151, 152, 154, 158, 159, 161, 62, 163, 168
Turandot (Puccini) *95*, 149, 151, 152, 153, 154, 155, 157, 158, 159, 160, 62, 168
Valkyrie, The (Wagner) 139 see also *Walküre*
Vespri siciliani, Le (Verdi) 150, 161
Vestale, La (Spontini) 150
Viaggio a Reims, Il (Rossini) 159
Villi, Le (Puccini) 159
Vogelhändler, Der (Zeller) 160
Walküre, Die (Wagner) *139*, 157, 161, 168
Wally, La (Catalani) *32*, 150, 153, 162, 168
Werther (Massenet) *71*, 152, 153, 154
West Side Story (Bernstein) *26*, 68
William Tell (Rossini) 155, 158
Yeomen of the Guard, The (Sullivan) *117*
Zarewitsch, Der (Lehár) 160
Zauberflöte, Die (Mozart) 77, *79*, *168*
Zazà (Leoncavallo) 156
Zigeunerbaron, Der (J Strauss)

RECOMMENDED RETAILERS

ADELAIDE
Don's Music
(Don Krahenbuhl)
Shop 18, Adelaide Arcade
Adelaide SA 5000
(08) 223 5892

John Davis Music
(Les Walker)
Twin Plaza, 22 Twin Street
Adelaide SA 5000
(08) 223 6369

Blockbuster Music
(Karen Tinman)
Shop R40 Myer Centre
Rundle Mall
Adelaide SA 5000
(08) 410 0433

BRISBANE
Harlequin Music Store
(Chris Warner)
Shop 43
Indooroopilly Shoppingtown
Indooroopilly QLD 4068
(07) 378 8888

The Record Market
(John Simpson)
52 Queen Street
Brisbane QLD 4000
(07) 210 0333

CANBERRA
Abels Music
(Ross Gengos)
Franklin Street
Manuka ACT 2603
(06) 295 1466

The Music Room
(Geoff Forgie)
The Canberra Centre
Bunda Street
Canberra ACT 2601
(06) 248 8390

HOBART
Eduardo's (Sandy Bay Hi-Fi)
(Nigel Dreaver)
9 Gregory Street
Sandy Bay TAS 7003
(002) 343 121

LAUNCESTON
Wills Music
(Kevin Leslie)
7 The Quadrant
Launceston TAS 7250
(003) 315 688

MELBOURNE
Myer Melbourne
(John Cross)
295 Lonsdale Street
Melbourne VIC 3000
(03) 9661 3465

Readings
(Max Peterson)
153 Toorak Road
South Yarra VIC 3141
(03) 9867 1885

Thomas' Pty Ltd
(Peter Posarnig)
31 Bourke Street
Melbourne Vic 3141
(03) 9650 2403

Virgin Megastore
(Philip Richards)
152–158 Bourke Street
Melbourne VIC 3000
(03) 9663 5277

PERTH
Gramophone Record
(Jim Richards)
Shop 16, Shafto Lane
876 Hay Street
Perth WA 6000
(09) 322 4341

Wesley Classics
(David Mold)
Shop 6, Wesley Arcade
Perth WA 6000
(09) 321 1978

SYDNEY
Angus & Robertson Bookworld
Classical Music Lounge
(Elizabeth Cubit)
Imperial Arcade
Pitt Street Mall
Sydney NSW 2000
(02) 221 5265

Blockbuster Classics
(George Cooks)
Sky Garden
162 Pitt Street
Sydney NSW 2000
(02) 223 8563

HMV — Mid City
(Vincent Dalgarno)
Shop 001
Mid City Centre
Pitt Street Mall
Sydney NSW 2000
(02) 221 2311

Mall Classics
(Forbes Cowper)
Shop 52, Warringah Mall
Brookvale NSW 2100
(02) 905 6588

Michael's Music Room
(Michael McNamara)
Shop 19, Town Hall Arcade
Sydney NSW 2000
(02) 267 1351

New Zealand
AUCKLAND
Marbeck's Records
15 Queens Arcade
Queens Street
Auckland
(09) 379 0451

WELLINGTON
Parsons Books and Music
126 Lambton Quay
Wellington
(04) 472 4587

CHRISTCHURCH
The CD Store
Big Fresh Shopping Centre
Cnr Madras Street
& Moorhouse Avenue
Christchurch
(03) 366 7097